Ann Ladbury's

Guide to

Simple

Pattern Cutting

Ann Ladbury's Guide to Simple Pattern Cutting

Ann Ladbury

B.T. Batsford Limited·London

© Ann Ladbury 1986
First published 1986

ISBN 0 7134 4341 3 (cased)

Typeset by Katerprint Typesetting Services, Oxford
and printed in Great Britain by
R J Acford Ltd
Chichester, Sussex

for the publishers
B. T. Batsford Ltd.
4 Fitzhardinge Street
London W1H 0AH

Contents

Acknowledgements

The original designs and adaptations were worked out by Janet Palmer who also did the pattern drawings. And this is another book that was typed by John through the BBC Micro. Long may it continue.

Dedication

I shall dedicate this book to Roger, my Bank Manager, who pointedly wrote on his Christmas card to me, '. . . may your pen never run dry'.

Introduction

You may be one of those people who can never find exactly what you want in the commercial pattern catalogues; maybe you have figure problems that would make it worthwhile cutting your own patterns; maybe you would just like to know how to change a style by having a different collar, putting in pleats etc. Whichever it is, this is the book for you. I have set out to show you in the simplest possible way, with straightforward, sensible instructions and without any mathematical calculations, how you can draft your own patterns.

There are a few basic principles to grasp and a few rules to follow. You will find it slow going at first but you will soon get the hang of it.

The basic pattern included is for women, in the size range that is known as 'Misses' in the commercial catalogues. The garments illustrated are adaptations of the bodice, sleeve, skirt and trousers but the principles of the adaptations apply to all, including children, so once you are familiar with the techniques you will be able to apply them to other patterns.

The sections on skirts and trousers come first because they are the simplest. I have added a brief order of sewing to these as a guide for less experienced dressmakers. It wasn't possible to do this for the bodice section because it would always be part of a garment such as dress, blouse etc.

With the help of this book you can cut stylish patterns to fit you, combining any features you wish and once you are confident about it you will find it quicker than making the trip out to buy a pattern. And cheaper.

It is a very enjoyable practical skill and it gives you a wonderful opportunity to express your design talents.

HOW TO USE THIS BOOK

Take your bust and hip measurements, consult the size chart on page 4 and decide what size basic block pattern will be best for you. Be honest in your choice: remember that the blocks allow the customary small ease allowance but not the larger amounts added to comply with fashion demands and included when you buy a commercial pattern. If it happens that you choose your usual size but you find that it is either small because you are fleshy and rely on more ease, or large because you are small-boned, nothing is lost because you have the other sizes in the book.

Select the size remembering that you can use a different bodice size from your skirt or trousers if your measurements indicate that it would be wise. Make a copy of each piece of block in your size. Do this by tracing it off onto soft sew-in Vilene/Pellon, or on paper, or on a length of thin cotton material. Transfer all markings using felt pen. DO NOT CUT UP THE MULTI-SIZE TISSUE unless you are sure you are going for the correct size and you are positive that you will never change size.

Next fit the block patterns and adjust for your figure problems if necessary. Follow the instructions on pages 8–18 for this. Finally, read the introductory sections of the book so that you understand the terminology and what equipment you will be using, look at the fashion sketches and then make a start. It is worth remembering that skirts are the easiest patterns to cut. Also, within each section the patterns are arranged in order of complexity so the simplest designs come first.

ABBREVIATIONS

I dislike abbreviations in the normal way but as this is a practical book and not one to sit and read through, I have tried to make it quicker for you to follow by abbreviating the following words:

Centre Back	CB
Centre Front	CF
Straight Grain	SG
Bust Point	BP
Centimetre	cm
Inch	in

MEASUREMENTS

Throughout the book metric measurements are used followed by the equivalent Imperial measurement. Use one system or the other.

Designing

It is quite likely that when you start you will have difficulty in planning a design. Try to think of something interesting to draft the pattern for but not so elaborate that you won't have time to make it up, or so bizarre that you won't be able to wear it. Whatever you decide on, you must be sure it will suit both your style of dressing and your figure. You must find a design and a fabric that look good on you and that look good when combined.

Use an illustration of some kind to copy. This can be a fashion sketch, a picture from a magazine, a newspaper sketch or one of the sketches in this book. Eventually you will be able to make your own fashion sketches. Start a collection of pictures showing various features, ideas for pockets, collars, pleats. Look at ready-made clothes to see what new techniques are being used, to see where the seams are, what the proportions are. See how the fabric has been used – gathered, pleated, on the bias etc.

It will be frustrating to draft a pattern for something only to find that the fabric is not available or your chosen fastening is nowhere to be found. Keep an eye on what is in the shops; look at good market stalls for interesting things; send for mail order swatches. Consider the purpose of the garment; fullness in sports clothes etc. Consider the width of the fabric; try not to make pattern pieces slightly too big to fit on the fabric. Either make them smaller or go for something fuller and have a seam.

It can be difficult to judge how the garment will look until you have had plenty of practice. One tip that will help you is to watch the width around the hem – measure hems of existing clothes to guide you. Also remember your height, you may not be average. And, finally, follow the old rule and flatter your good points with decorative features and emphasis, in order to play down your non-average areas.

Equipment

You must have certain items of special equipment in addition to the obvious things that will be around the house. It is better to collect the correct equipment, for, as with all practical work this makes it so much easier to do.

You will need pencils, rubber, pins, tape-measure, sellotape and scissors for cutting paper; the Pikaby glue-stick for paper is useful too. In addition buy a spiked tracing-wheel – the plain wheel is for use with dressmaker's carbon paper for making continuous lines on fabric. Two other items are a flexible curve, which is a pliable rubbery stick that you can shape to any curve. It is not essential but very useful if your freehand curves are not good – obtainable from stationery shops. And you must also have a metre rule or measuring stick. This can be made of wood or metal. Make sure it is marked in centimetres or inches (depending on the system of measurement you have selected), at least along the edge that you will use most, reading from left to right along upper edge. Use it for ruling all straight lines.

Card: After adjusting the block patterns cut them out in durable card, perhaps using different colours for each piece. They will get a lot of use because you will have to draw round them each time you make a pattern. Label each one clearly and store together by hanging them up. Punch a hole in each and put a loop of string through and hang up on a hook or a coat hanger.

Paper: You need a lot of paper that is strong enough to last until after pinning to the fabric and maybe longer, but not so heavy it is awkward to use. It is also more useful if you can see through it. You might want to begin by using wallpaper lining paper or greaseproof paper or brown parcel paper but eventually you will want to use plain white pattern paper. You may find this in specialist shops but it is also available by post. See page 120 for details.

I have not recommended the use of squared pattern paper in this book. The lines can be confusing and it is not easy to see pencil lines. You will find it much easier in the end to use plain paper, making use of the edges and corners, and you will feel less restricted when drawing curves etc., and adding seam allowances. However, if you haven't got a cutting board (which incidentally I only use for cutting out and sewing, never for pattern cutting) a few sheets of squared paper are useful for laying out your pattern to calculate fabric quantity.

Table: Finally, you need somewhere smooth and flat to do the pattern cutting. The tracing wheel will damage the dining table but you can protect it with a sheet of chipboard or hardboard. An excellent alternative is a wallpaper pasting table but if it really gets used for that purpose make sure the owner doesn't mind a few holes in the surface.

Collect also, each time you start a pattern, a few small heavy objects to use to weight each pattern as it needs outlining. It is much quicker and more accurate than pinning pieces together. Use kitchen weights, paper weights, pebbles, toys etc.

THE MULTI-SIZE BASIC BLOCKS

Included with this book is a set of basic blocks, multi-sized from 10–20. They have no style or fashion lines, they are simple body shapes fitted with darts. There are no collars or facings, no pockets or pleats. Use the shapes provided, following the instructions in the book, to create your own styles, adding what you want in the way of features and decoration. The basic blocks include:

Bodice	Back: Shoulder dart, waist dart. Front: Underarm dart, waist dart.
Sleeve	Full length; elbow dart.
Straight skirt	Back: Two darts. Front: One dart.
A-Line skirt	Back: One dart. Front: One dart.
Trousers	Back: Two darts. Front: One dart.

SIZE CHART FOR BUST AND HIPS

MEASUREMENTS(CM/IN)

SIZES	10	12	14	16	18	20
BUST	84/33	88/34$\frac{3}{4}$	92/36$\frac{1}{4}$	96/37$\frac{3}{4}$	100/39$\frac{1}{4}$	104/41
HIPS	90/35$\frac{1}{2}$	94/37	98/38$\frac{1}{2}$	102/40	106/41$\frac{3}{4}$	110/43$\frac{1}{4}$

Seam Allowances

Please note that the basic blocks have no seam allowances.

When drafting patterns you must work with a net pattern knowing that the edges are seam lines. You can then cut and spread pieces, insert extra where needed, add extensions etc. You can also judge more clearly where your style features such as yokes, will really fall on the garment. It also means that you can work with much greater accuracy, measuring and checking edges etc.

Most people, I believe, like to have seam and hem allowances on a pattern when they pin it to the fabric. For this reason I have included the instructions to add them to final patterns in the book. However, professionals work without seam allowances, and if you have used Burda patterns you will know the benefit of this. It enables you to be more economical in fabric; it means that you can add only what is necessary at a particular point in a specific fabric. For example, 1cm ($\frac{3}{8}$in) or even less is quite sufficient on collars and pockets. Why not try using patterns without seam allowances? Whatever you decide to do, **don't forget to add seam allowances**, either on the pattern or on the fabric.

Balance Marks or Notches

These are vital points used at pattern edges to indicate where pieces meet. Make your personal blocks in card, transferring all the markings including balance marks. Cut out the personal blocks and snip a V into the card at every balance mark – now literally a 'notch'. You can buy a tool for clipping pattern edges which is worth having if you do a lot of pattern drafting. Each time you trace or copy a block or pattern, transfer every notch with a pencil mark. On the final pattern pieces you can clip them if you wish.

Whenever you cut through a pattern piece in the course of producing your final pattern, draw the cutting line, yoke, pleat, new neckline etc., then make one or two pencil strokes across the line. When you cut along the line both cut edges will have a pencil mark. Continue transferring these new balance marks to the final pattern.

You will know that commercial patterns have armholes marked with a single balance mark or notch on the front, and with two on the back. If you keep to this on all pattern pieces it will make it easier for you to distinguish front and back patterns at a glance. Do it on such things as collars and pockets too, one for the front, two for the back.

USING THE BLOCK PATTERNS

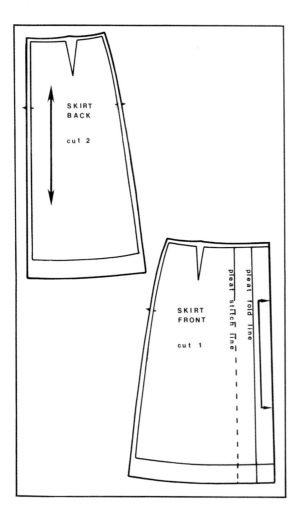

Always make copies of the block; never cut up or alter the original blocks. Even if you want to make a basic change for weight loss or hem length, make a new block keeping the original for reference.

Copy the block by placing it on paper and outlining it in pencil, including the darts and notches. Remove the block. Mark each with name of piece immediately.

Select your design from the section of the book which begins on page 19 and make the necessary adaptations for the style you choose. If the adaptation involves cutting the pattern and inserting more paper for pleats, gathers etc., you may have to outline it yet again on another piece of paper. Having completed the pattern, mark edges to be placed to the fold of fabric with arrows or write the word FOLD, draw straight grain lines on other pieces. Add 1.5cm ($\frac{5}{8}$in) seam allowance on seam edges, or more if you prefer, add a hem allowance of about 6–8cm ($2\frac{1}{2}$–$3\frac{3}{4}$in) for a conventional hem in most fabrics; add 1cm ($\frac{3}{8}$in) on a circular or flared style; add 3cm ($1\frac{1}{4}$in) if fabric is suitable for a Wundaweb/Stitch Witchery/Save-a-Stitch hem. If the hem is to be bound then no allowance is necessary. Write the amount of seam and hem allowance clearly on the pattern pieces as a reminder. Transfer the notches to the outer edge of the pattern piece. For clarity, these are shown on the illustrations as extending triangles but they can be made with pencil strokes within the pattern edge.

Add any other information needed to help in making up, remembering that it may well be some time before you finish with the pattern. Mark each CUT 1, CUT 2 etc. Finally draw the correct shape across the ends of the darts by folding the paper and pinning the dart with the bulk in the correct direction ie., towards centre of body or downwards. Mark across paper using a toothed tracing wheel, remove pins, flatten the paper and the correct outline is revealed by a line of holes.

Cut out the pattern pieces ready for use.

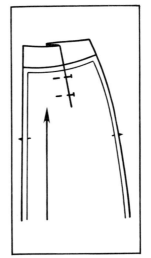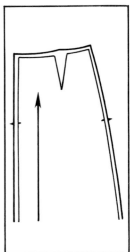

Pattern Edges

One of the advantages of working without seam allowances is that you can make sure your finished pattern is accurate.

Make a final check of all seam edges that meet, before adding on seam and hem allowances. Place them together with edges meeting to make sure they are equal in length and also, with straight edges. Make sure they touch all the way along. Check that the balance marks are opposite each other; move them if necessary.

Next put pairs of pattern pieces on top of each other with edges together as though you were going to make a seam. Check the edges, remembering that the edges represent the stitching line. Check the balance marks. Do this to all pieces, including folding cuff to see if ends meet; placing collars to necklines, standing the collar on edge for accuracy.

If you find a discrepancy move one piece of pattern slightly and trim a little from each end of the longer piece. Check curves to see that they are smooth and continuous. For example check the neckline curve by placing front and back patterns together at shoulders with neck edges together. Check that the back runs smoothly into the front. Re-draw and re-cut if necessary. The illustration shows projecting points as dotted lines, re-draw as a smooth curve.

Check armholes by placing pattern together at armhole edge. Re-draw and re-cut if necessary.

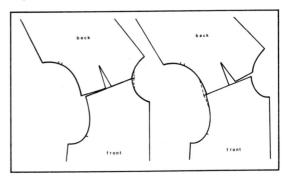

FITTING
Measuring

You need two measurements to help you to decide what size basic pattern to use.

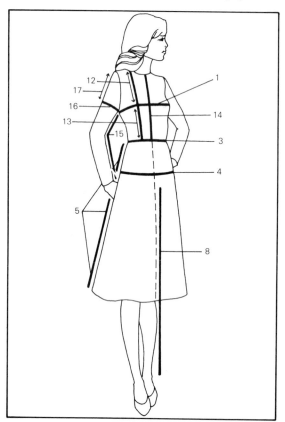

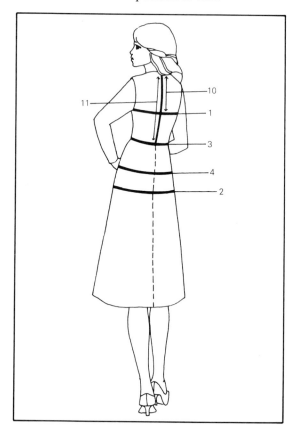

Bust: Run tape measure round over fullest part of bust, over underwear (1). Choose bodice and sleeve pattern in nearest size.

Hips: Pass tape measure round figure 15cm (6in) below waist (2). Choose skirts and trousers by this measurement.

If you have wide hips below that point, or big thighs, treat this as a fitting problem when trying on the pattern and add extra from hip line level to hem. If you are very pear-shaped you will not be needing the straight skirt at all.

If you know you have a fitting problem make a copy of the appropriate piece of basic pattern and fit it and adjust it as described in the following sections.

Preparing Basic Pattern for Fitting

Trace off each piece using soft sew-in Vilene/Pellon or a length of thin soft fabric. Mark darts, balance marks and SG lines with felt pen. Cut out the pieces for the right half of the body adding a seam allowance all round to make it easier to handle the pieces.

You can if you wish, cut out all the pieces in experimental fabric such as thin cotton or sheeting and baste up whole trousers, skirt, bodice and sleeve and fit and adjust each one. It is a particularly good idea with trousers as faults are less easy to put right after they have been cut in the final fabric.

After adjusting the pattern, transfer all alterations to the basic pattern and make cardboard blocks ready to use for making your designs.

Fitting and Adjusting

Work through the following, selecting those that you think apply to your figure. Some checks can be made by measuring the pattern, others are best done by pinning the piece to the body. As you adjust them, excess should be pinned or stitched; where there is a shortage either cut the pattern and insert extra or pin extra to the edge or, at hems, simply write it on the pattern and add it when making the cardboard blocks. Use the guide lines on the basic pattern to establish the correct position for altering each pattern piece.

After adjusting check that corresponding edges are correct in length and check curves and ends of darts to make sure the shape is right.

It is worth spending time fitting the basic patterns because your blocks will then convert into patterns, and therefore garments that will fit.

SKIRT

Mark waistline by tying a piece of tape round (3). Pin front skirt to figure with waist in position and CF vertical. Pleat pattern above hip line (4) to bring pattern to correct depth of hip (A). Fold dart into position, check length and width (A). Folds below waist indicate tight darts; creases at dart ends indicate darts too long (B). Repeat with back skirt. If you have a

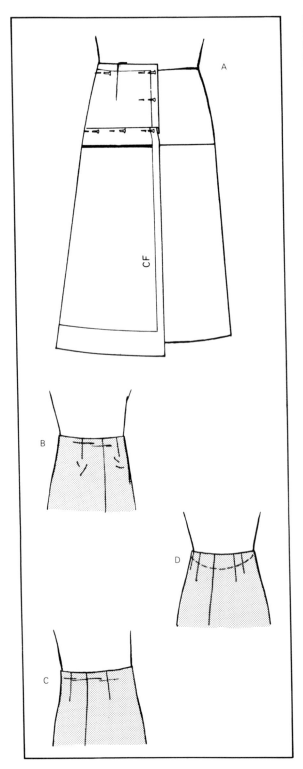

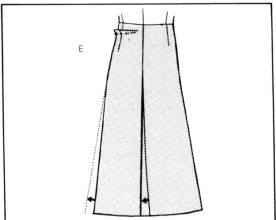

hollow back, shown by folds across back below waist, you will need to make a complete back pattern as the problem may not be evident on half a pattern (C). Smooth pattern above waist to remove wrinkles. Re-draw new lower waistline to follow natural waist (D). One or two darts can be used, it depends on relationship between waist and hip size.

With back and front in position check that side seams hang straight. Lift skirt at front or back waist to correct (E). If skirt is tight over hips or thighs, insert extra paper. Check skirt length, adjust pattern at line above hem (5).

TROUSERS

Check pattern by measuring, starting with crotch depth. Pass tape round crotch from back waist to front (6). Pin pattern pieces together at crotch and check seam length.

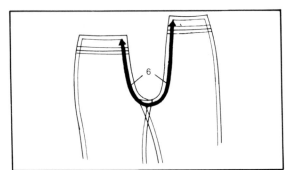

Adjust pattern by folding along line below waist or by cutting and inserting extra paper.

Measure outside leg length (7). Measure inside leg length (8). Check pattern in both places and adjust at line below knee.

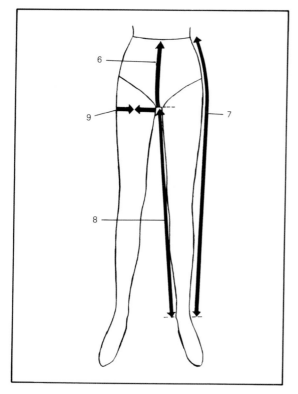

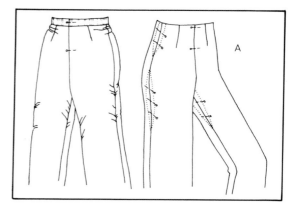

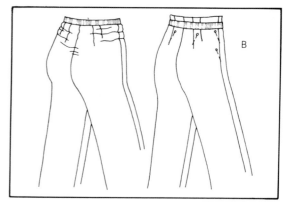

Measure thigh (9). Check pattern; allow plenty of ease. To make pattern smaller, pleat from waist to hem; to make it larger, add on from hip to hem or use larger pattern.

If you fit a whole pair of trousers you may find it easier to keep them in position if you baste a length of curved petersham to the waistline.

Look at the following areas and correct any of the problems described. If trousers are tight at waist or hip, release side seam where necessary. Make sure side seam is not crooked; it is often better to release the inside leg seam to give more ease over thighs (A). If trouser waist rises above natural waist remove petersham, smooth fabric above waist, re-pin darts to new length (B). Trousers that are tight

across the crotch show wrinkles across the legs and sometimes below the waist. Release the inside leg seam, possibly letting out crotch seam. Release crotch seam below waist if necessary (C). If the trousers are tight across the bottom, showing creases under crotch and below waist, release the back crotch seam and

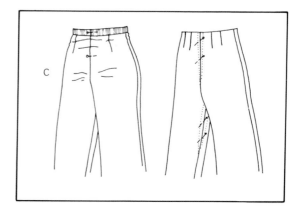

inside leg seam. If this is not enough, release side seam (D). The most common problem of all is that of loose, baggy folds under the bottom that no amount of lifting will cure (E). Re-shape the entire crotch seam by lowering it slightly across the inside leg seam and scooping out the back below the crotch. Shape the seam back to original line. The trousers can now be lifted but the waist will be loose so take in back crotch seam from waist to start of new curve. Check trouser length as this alteration shortens the legs.

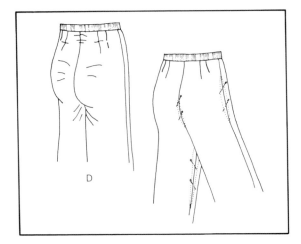

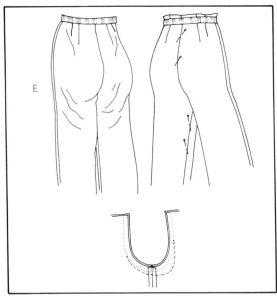

BODICE

Back: Measure from back neck to underarm (10). The easiest way to do this is to hold a ruler under one arm against your back and get someone to take the measurement (A). Check

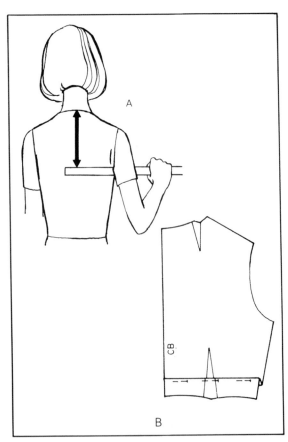

the pattern and adjust at the back shoulder line on the pattern. Measure from underarm to waist at CB (11). Check pattern, adjust at line above waist (B). If you have a hollow back it is quite likely that your waistline dips at CB and you need extra length there but not at the side seam. If this is so cut the pattern almost to the side, open it up and insert extra paper. Redraw straight dart and CB line (C).

Next fit the shoulders and neck. Pin back pattern to figure. Fold out the shoulder dart and smooth it to the figure, pin pattern at CB

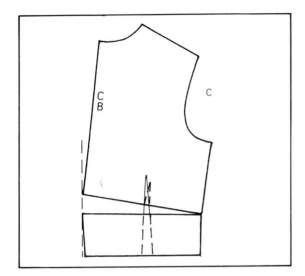

and underarm, pin out waist dart. If you have square shoulders or straight back the dart can remain in the shoulder but many people find a neck dart more comfortable, especially if the back of the figure is rounded. Like all darts this one should be directed towards the bulge

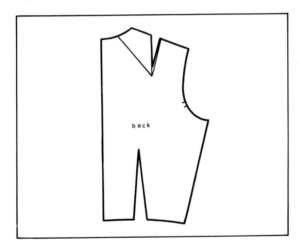

of the figure. It can of course be used in the neck for some designs and in the shoulder for others. To transfer the dart to the neck cut the pattern on the line shown; cut out the shoulder dart extending it right to the point. Close the shoulder dart to allow it to open up in the neckline. Draw the neck dart 5cm (2in) long. Fold the dart out, smoothing the paper

towards CB and cut along neckline. Open out to reveal correctly shaped edge. A figure with a rounded back will require extra length between neck and underarm. Cut along back line and open pattern to insert wedge of paper. Remove pattern and make sure it lies flat before making permanent alteration. Straighten CB edge. If this makes back neck too wide, make neck dart a little bigger (D).

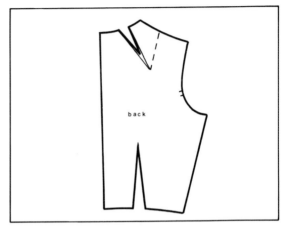

Check back width of pattern above armhole. If it is too wide take a pleat from shoulder grading it to nothing at waist. If too tight let in a small amount at the same point (E). If only a little is needed, re-draw the armhole slightly straighter (F). If back neck is too wide reduce

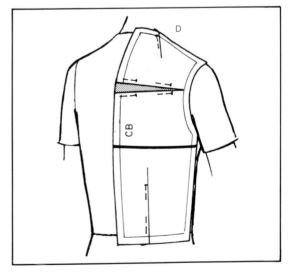

at shoulder point by re-drawing shoulder seam (G). If too narrow, raise shoulder seam and re-draw neckline (H).

For a figure that is fleshy underarm, the 'spare tyre' causing wrinkling across the blade, shorten the darts or change them to short tucks or gathers (I).

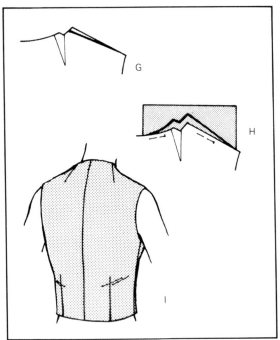

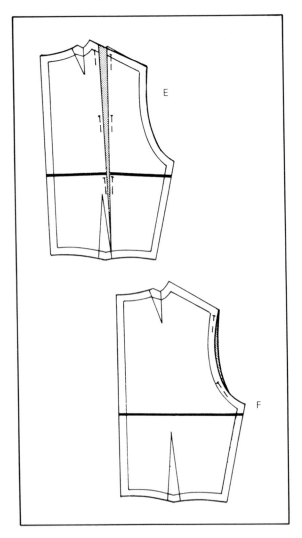

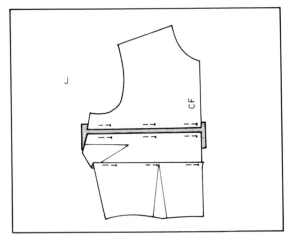

underarm level or by cutting and inserting more paper (J, K). You may then have to compensate by adding or reducing by the same amount at the line below the bust but before doing so measure the figure from BP to waist and check the pattern (13). Also take the total measurement from neck to waist and check (14).

If the amount by which the point of the dart needs moving up or down to fit the true bust,

Front: Fit the front pattern by measuring or by pinning to the figure or using a combination of both.

Measure from shoulder to BP (12). Check pattern. Shorten or lengthen the pattern above the bust line by folding out the surplus at

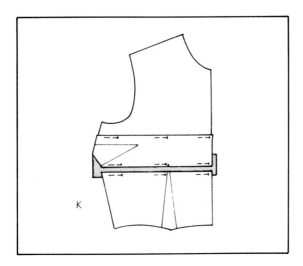

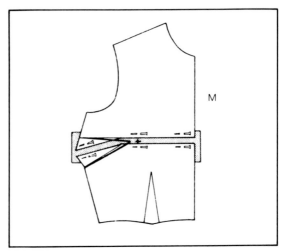

is very slight, it can be done more easily by simply re-drawing the dart (L).

If you know from your bra cup size, or from previous experience that the usual bust dart is insufficient, cut the pattern along the dart and along the bust line. Separate the pieces and insert an even amount of extra paper between

If you know you have square or sloping shoulders or if you usually have problems fitting the neck you will need to put on a complete bodice, joined at the shoulders.

Check that the shoulder seams run straight, not to front or back. For square shoulders release shoulder seam at armhole edge. For

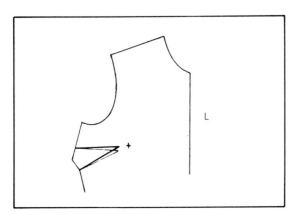

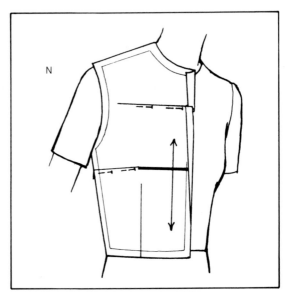

the edges. About 1–2cm ($\frac{5}{8}$–$\frac{3}{4}$in) is usually required. Draw a new dart, wider at the base. Fold the dart and re-cut the pattern edge (M).

A hollow or narrow chest should be corrected on the figure by folding out the surplus on the chest line or by folding back surplus paper from neckline, graduating to nothing below the bust (N). This creates a new CF line. Spread the pattern flat and rule the new straight edge.

sloping shoulders lift the seam. If in doubt undo the seam, lift edges and re-pin a new seam (O).

Neck fitting problems are usually the result of posture. If the neck slopes forward, lower the front neckline and raise the back (P). If the figure is erect there will be excess at the back neck. Remove this by taking more out of shoulder seams, by shaping the CB seam or by inserting a neck dart. You may also find you will have to re-shape the front neck (Q).

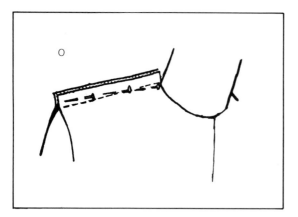

If the neckline chokes you it may be due to a neck with a broad base. This may be cured by lowering it but a better solution may be to insert an extra piece of paper in the shoulder seam (R). Re-curve the edges and re-draw the seam line. You are probably now beginning to

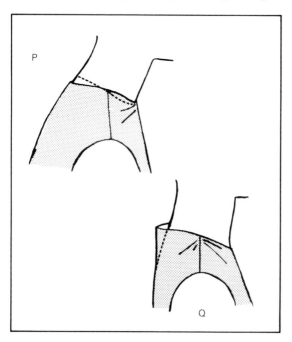

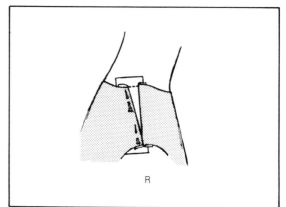

see the value of having a block that fits and of drafting your own collars etc., to fit the block.

Sleeve: Measure the arm from wrist to underarm, or measure a garment (15). Check the pattern but do not alter until you have found out whether it should be lengthened or shortened above or below the elbow. You may know which from experience but if not, baste up a sleeve and try it on. Alter the pattern to fit.

Measure round the top of the arm and check the pattern width (16). A small extra amount can be added by letting out the seam (A). If more is required cut the pattern along the vertical central line and across it at underarm level. Open out the pieces to insert a little in the width but keeping all pieces flat and joined at outer edges of sleeve. Re-cut the sleeve. Other small changes to width at elbow or wrist level can be made by adjusting the seam (B, C). One final check that is useful although you may not observe the results of the problem until you have the sleeve attached to the bodice, involves measuring from top of arm to underarm level (17). Check the pattern depth at that point. Any substantial difference is usually the result of having square or sloping shoulders. The sleeve heads can be made deeper by scooping out the underarm curve (D), or shallower by taking a little off the top (E). Keep curves a good shape and check sleeve length afterwards as it will have altered.

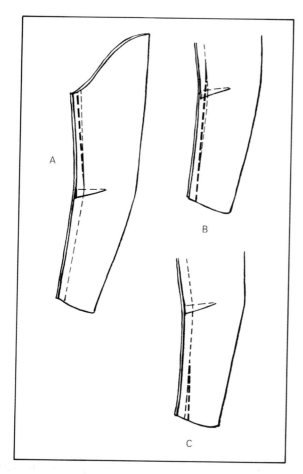

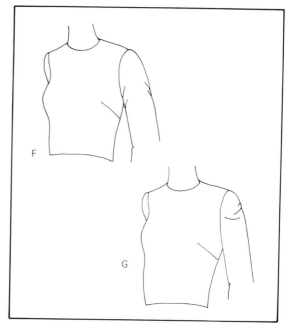

When the sleeve is in the bodice the result of a sleeve head being too shallow is shown in illustration (F) and the result of a deep one in illustration (G).

Note

Having altered your basic pattern, check all seam edges and curves for accuracy. Trim off all seam allowances and make your cardboard blocks. Keep all your experimental pieces; they always make a useful reference.

Note

The numbers in square brackets in the text of this chapter refer to the numbers printed on the illustrations on page 8.

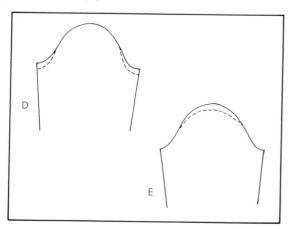

ROUTINE

There is a correct and logical way of working that begins with the internal shaping and ends with the edges. In order not to waste paper begin by establishing the length – hip, knee, ankle, short or long sleeve etc., and use the block to that length.

1. Outline block of main pattern piece.
2. Establish shaping by moving darts etc.
3. Add any style lines such as yokes and cut block.
4. Work on each piece separately, inserting fullness for gathers etc.
5. Adapt neckline and armhole of bodices. Draft facings.
6. Adapt for openings.
7. Draft collars, pockets etc.
8. Mark SG, CF, CB, FOLD as appropriate on all pieces. Name each piece.
9. Re-cut, adding seam and hem allowances.

You will often be using the basic block as it is, especially trousers or back skirt or bodice, but always make a paper pattern; never just use the block on the fabric.

CHECK LIST

Before you cut round your final pattern outline check the following:

1. Have you added seam and hem allowances?
2. Have you checked that seam edges that meet are the same length?
3. Are all the FOLD edges marked?
4. Are the straight grain arrows there?
5. Check the pattern with the previous stage to make sure you haven't inadvertently left out a dart or something.
6. Are all the balance marks transferred to final pattern?
7. Are all the pieces named?
8. Are all the pices marked CUT 1, CUT 2 etc.?
9. Have you got an envelope ready marked for storing the pattern, showing a sketch and the size?

FASHION SKETCHES

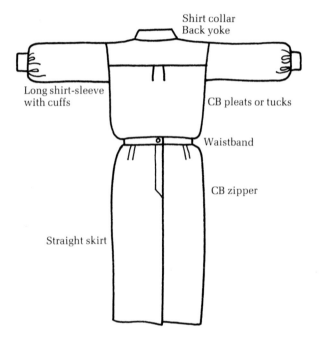

Shirt collar
Back yoke

Long shirt-sleeve
with cuffs

CB pleats or tucks

Waistband

CB zipper

Straight skirt

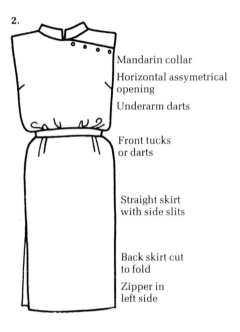

2.

Mandarin collar

Horizontal assymetrical
opening

Underarm darts

Front tucks
or darts

Straight skirt
with side slits

Back skirt cut
to fold

Zipper in
left side

Long sleeve gathered into cuff

Double-breasted opening

A-line panel skirt

Dart transferred to yoke gathers

Zipper in left side

Seam pockets in panel

'Eton' style collar

Plain short sleeve

Patch pocket
Underarm dart

Waistband
Zipper at side or CB

A-line skirt; inverted pleat at front

Low round neck back and front; no opening required

Flared sleeve

Bust shaping in waist

Zipper in side or CB

Skirt with moderate flare

V-neck with bias collar and tie ends

Underarm dart

Long sleeve gathered into cuff

Zipper at side or back seam

A-line skirt cut in 4 gores

Cut panels on bias of striped fabric

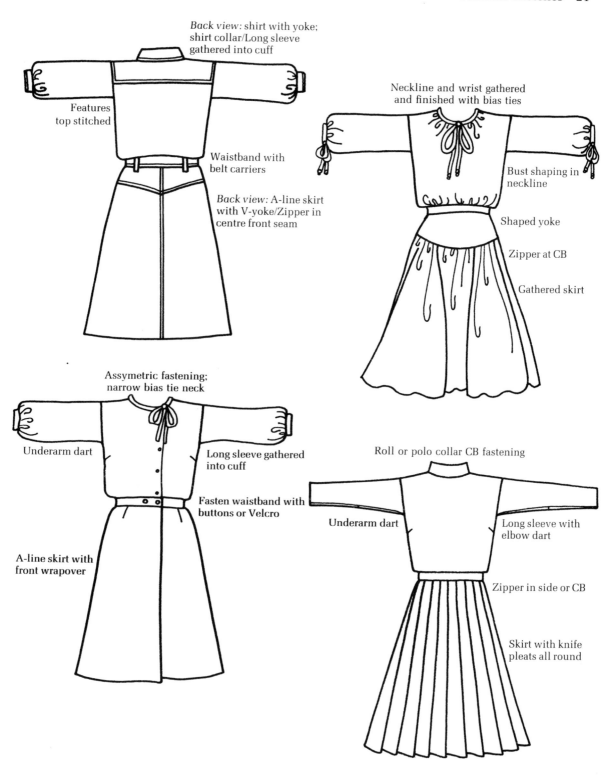

Back view: shirt with yoke; shirt collar/Long sleeve gathered into cuff

Features top stitched

Waistband with belt carriers

Back view: A-line skirt with V-yoke/Zipper in centre front seam

Neckline and wrist gathered and finished with bias ties

Bust shaping in neckline

Shaped yoke

Zipper at CB

Gathered skirt

Assymetric fastening; narrow bias tie neck

Underarm dart

Long sleeve gathered into cuff

Fasten waistband with buttons or Velcro

A-line skirt with front wrapover

Roll or polo collar CB fastening

Underarm dart

Long sleeve with elbow dart

Zipper in side or CB

Skirt with knife pleats all round

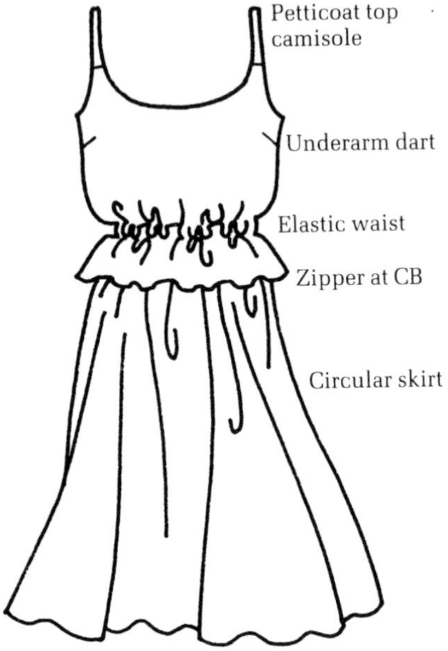

Petticoat top
camisole

Underarm dart

Elastic waist

Zipper at CB

Circular skirt

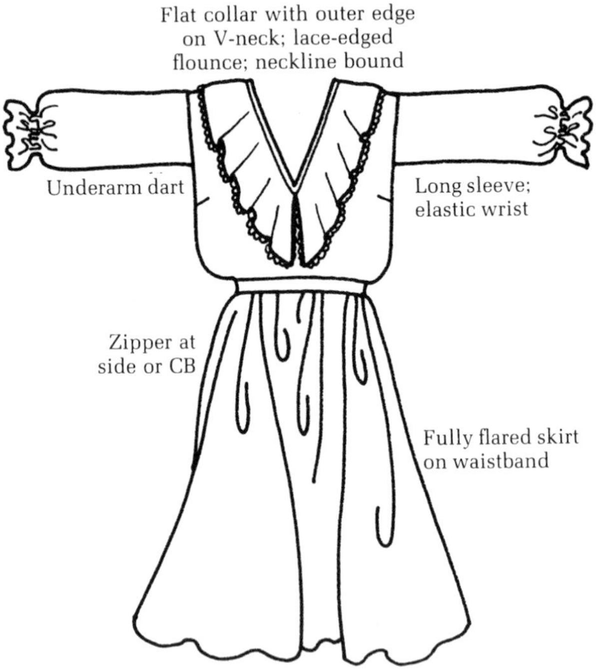

Flat collar with outer edge
on V-neck; lace-edged
flounce; neckline bound

Underarm dart

Long sleeve;
elastic wrist

Zipper at
side or CB

Fully flared skirt
on waistband

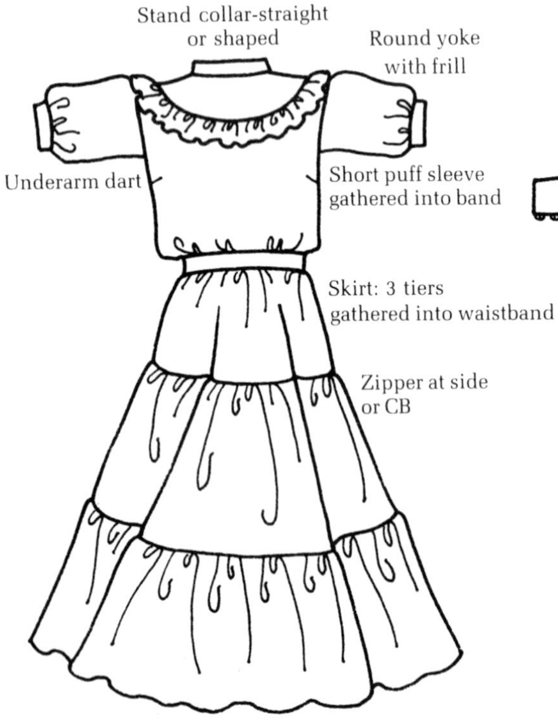

Stand collar-straight
or shaped

Round yoke
with frill

Underarm dart

Short puff sleeve
gathered into band

Skirt: 3 tiers
gathered into waistband

Zipper at side
or CB

Could be made into dress by omitting
waistband and joining skirt to top
at waist level, gathering to fit if
necessary. Attach stretched elastic
to seam allowance inside waist.

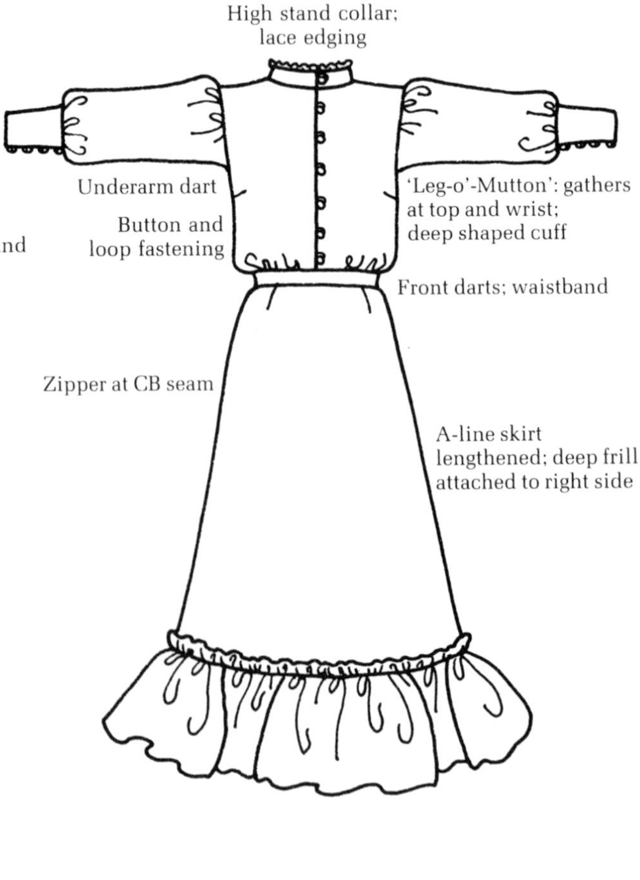

High stand collar;
lace edging

Underarm dart

Button and
loop fastening

'Leg-o'-Mutton': gathers
at top and wrist;
deep shaped cuff

Front darts; waistband

Zipper at CB seam

A-line skirt
lengthened; deep frill
attached to right side

Bound neckline

Underarm dart

Vertical tucks

Long or ¾ sleeve gathered at head; finished with narrow bias at hem or cuff band

Gathered skirt
Zipper at side or CB

Double frills at hem edge
Braid or ribbon strips or tucks above hem

Scooped neck back and front; may not require an opening

Elbow length sleeve, rolled up

Small patch pocket

Underarm dart

Inset pockets

Fly-front zipper

Tapered trousers

Ankle length

Low neck; back opening

Lowered armhole; cut away shoulder

High waist

Seam pockets stitched through garment

Flared skirt

Basic trousers; elastic waist

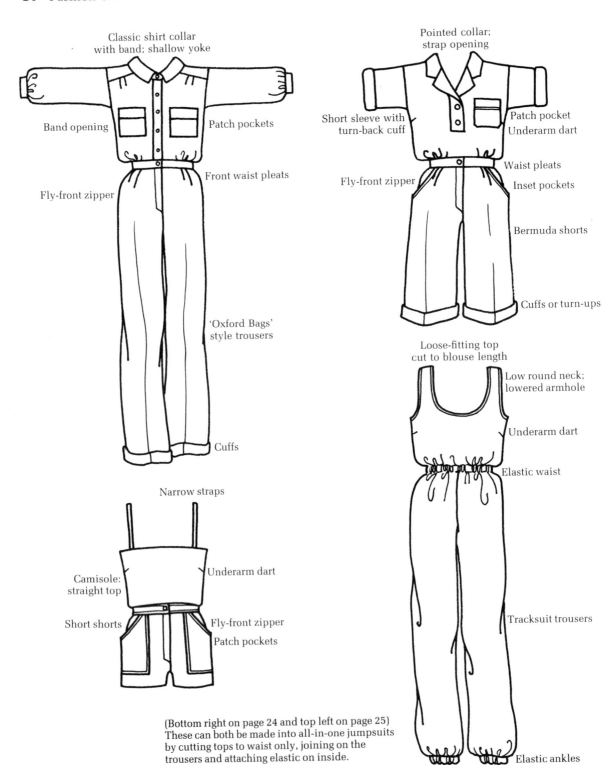

Classic shirt collar with band; shallow yoke

Band opening

Patch pockets

Front waist pleats

Fly-front zipper

'Oxford Bags' style trousers

Cuffs

Narrow straps

Camisole: straight top

Short shorts

Underarm dart

Fly-front zipper

Patch pockets

Pointed collar; strap opening

Short sleeve with turn-back cuff

Patch pocket

Underarm dart

Fly-front zipper

Waist pleats

Inset pockets

Bermuda shorts

Cuffs or turn-ups

Loose-fitting top cut to blouse length

Low round neck; lowered armhole

Underarm dart

Elastic waist

Tracksuit trousers

Elastic ankles

(Bottom right on page 24 and top left on page 25) These can both be made into all-in-one jumpsuits by cutting tops to waist only, joining on the trousers and attaching elastic on inside.

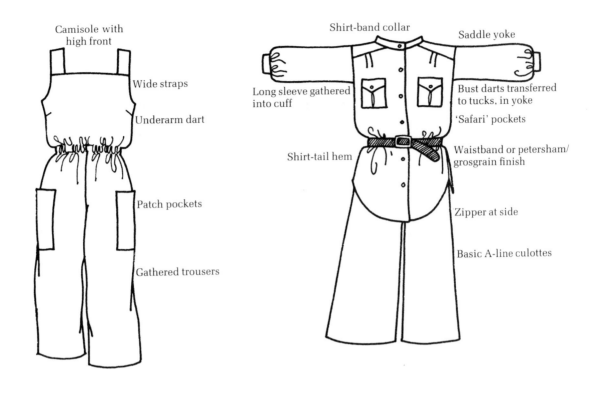

Camisole with
high front

Wide straps

Underarm dart

Patch pockets

Gathered trousers

Shirt-band collar

Saddle yoke

Long sleeve gathered
into cuff

Bust darts transferred
to tucks, in yoke

'Safari' pockets

Shirt-tail hem

Waistband or petersham/
grosgrain finish

Zipper at side

Basic A-line culottes

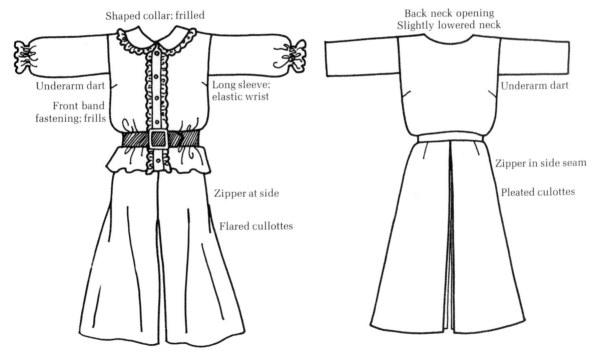

Shaped collar; frilled

Underarm dart

Front band
fastening; frills

Long sleeve;
elastic wrist

Zipper at side

Flared cullottes

Back neck opening
Slightly lowered neck

Underarm dart

Zipper in side seam

Pleated culottes

Round neck; back
zipper; sleeveless

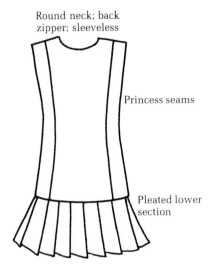

Princess seams

Pleated lower
section

V-neck; back neck
can be high or low
with CB zipper

Sleeveless;
faced or bound

Curved panel seams

Deep gathered
lower section

Short sleeve;
gathered head

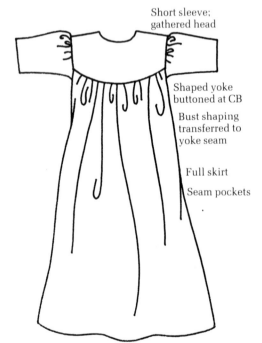

Shaped yoke
buttoned at CB

Bust shaping
transferred to
yoke seam

Full skirt

Seam pockets

Scooped neck; opening
on shoulder or at CB

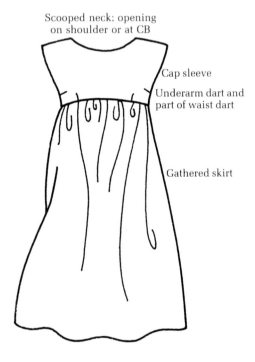

Cap sleeve

Underarm dart and
part of waist dart

Gathered skirt

V-neck with sailor collar
(flat collar)

Plain short sleeve

Underarm dart

Detachable bow

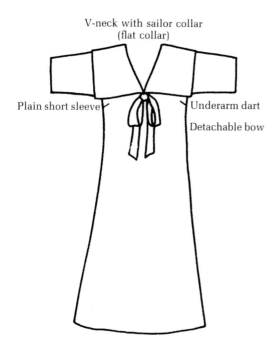

Shirt collar

Plain short sleeve

Patch pocket

Elastic in waist

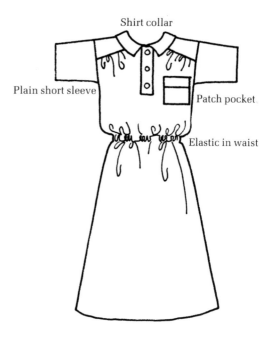

SKIRT DESIGNS
Straight Skirts

The basic straight skirt block has slightly sloping side seams and this shape is about as straight as it can be worn. Even then it only allows for sufficient walking room if the length is above the knee. If the block is used for a longer skirt it is necessary to insert a pleat or slit at the centre back, centre front or one, or both, sides.

(a) STRAIGHT SKIRT WITH CB SLIT OR PLEAT

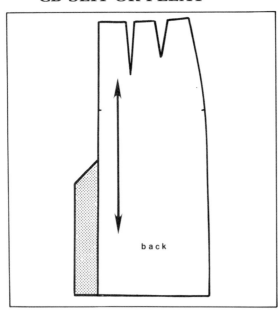

The adaptation for a pleat is the same as for a slit, the difference comes in the making up.

Back: Outline back skirt block. Decide on depth of slit of pleat, add an extra 8cm ($3\frac{1}{4}$in) to CB edge and slope back to seam edge as shown. Mark stitching point on CB seam at base of slope. Mark SG, add seam and hem allowance.

Front: Outline front skirt block, add seam and hem allowance, mark CF FOLD. Cut waistband.

Note
The same method can be used for a skirt with a CF pleat. The pattern could also be lengthened to floor length.

Making up
1. Stitch CB seam from base of zipper to top of pleat. Stitch from pleat up to waist and from pleat to hem using large straight machine stitch. Press seam open from waist to hem.
2. Press pleat extensions to one side, snipping the opposite seam allowance so that it lies flat.
3. Insert zipper.
4. With RS up stitch from CB seam through skirt and pleat.
5. Stitch back and front darts. Press.
6. Stitch and press side seams.
7. Attach waistband and fastening.

8. Turn up hem. For slit oversew hem edges together on both parts of slit. For pleat turn up hem with pleat seam open, press then snip seam at hem edge. Press.

(b) STRAIGHT SKIRT WITH SIDE SLIT

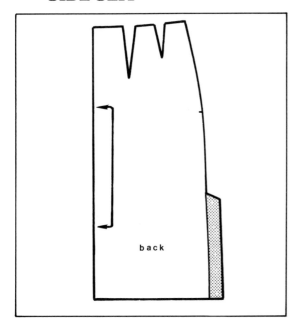

back

The illustration shows a skirt cut to a fold at CB and CF with zipper in left side seam but it could equally well be cut with a CB seam.

Back: Outline skirt block. Decide on depth of slit and add 5cm (2in) to side edge, sloping up to seam edge. Mark stitching point level with base of slope. Mark CB FOLD if appropriate. Add seam and hem allowance.

Front: As back. Mark CF FOLD. Cut waistband.

Making up
  1. Stitch CB seam and insert zipper if appropriate.
  2. Stitch back and front darts.
  3. Stitch side seam from slit point to waist. Stitch from slit point to hem with large stitch. Press open. If only one slit is required stitch the opposite seam from hem to waist, trim off extension and press. Insert zipper in left seam if appropriate.
  4. Attach waistband and fastening.
  5. Press light Fold-a-Band/Fuse'n'Fold/Waist-Shaper to WS from top of slit to hemline aligning perforations on fold.
  6. Turn up and stitch hem with extensions out. Fold extensions back, trim away bulk in hem. Press and loopstitch and slip stitch to hold extension to hem. Work bar-tack at top of slit. Press.

Note that this pattern could also be made into a skirt with pleats at the sides by pressing both extensions towards the front and stitching together.

A-Line Skirts

The A-line skirt block with its sloping side seams and single dart at back and front is a popular wearable style in itself. The block can be used without adapting to make a plain skirt of any length from mini to mid-calf, even floor length. The back can be cut with a CB seam and zipper, or the zipper can be put in the left seam; the front can be cut to the fold or with a CF seam, the latter could be topstitched and the skirt made with topstitched waistband and narrow hem. There are many possible variations.

To make a pattern, outline front and back blocks, mark FOLD at front or back wherever appropriate. Add seam and hem allowances and cut out.

(a) A-LINE SKIRT WITH CF INVERTED PLEAT

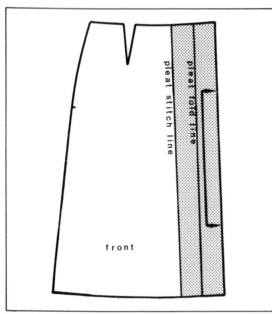

pleat stitch line

pleat fold line

front

The skirt illustrated shows the pleat top-stitched, but that could be omitted, the pleat could also be unpressed from waist, the zipper can be inserted in the side or CB seam.

Back: Outline A-line block, add seam and hem allowances. Cut out.

Back: Outline A-line block. Mark CB seam, add seam and hem allowances and cut out.

Front: Outline the A-line block. Rule a line parallel with CF edge 8cm (3¼in) away and a second line parallel with CF edge 8cm (3¼in) from it. Mark the outer line CF FOLD, the middle one PLEAT FOLD LINE and the inner one PLEAT STITCH LINE. Decide on depth of pleat and mark the stitch line at that point. Add seam and hem allowances but to obtain the correct hem edge fold the pleat into position and mark across the hem with a toothed tracing wheel in the same way as marking a dart edge. Cut waistband.

Making up

1. Stitch pleat on WS with a large stitch from hem to stitch point; stitch with normal stitch from there to waist. Press pleat. Top stitch if required.

2. Stitch CB seam; insert zipper if appropriate.

3. Insert back and front darts.

4. Stitch side seams.

5. Attach waistband and fastenings.

6. Press light Fold-a-Band/Fuse'n'Fold/Waist-Shaper to WS pleat with perforations aligned to outer fold. Turn up and finish hem. Press.

(b) A-LINE PANEL SKIRT

The back has a CB seam. The front has the panel and so it is cut to a fold. Seam pockets could be inserted into the front panel seams a little below the waistline. The zipper can be at

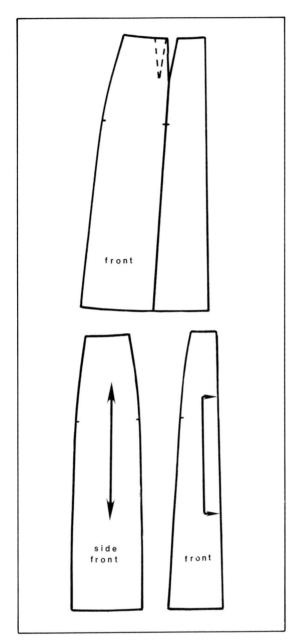

Front: Outline front block. Draw panel line from a point beside the dart to the hem, sloping it to make the panel slightly wider at the hem. The precise slope of the seam will form the style feature so it is for you to decide where to draw it. Do not make it straight or the panel will appear to be narrower at the hem. At the waist, transfer the dart into the panel by measuring it and re-drawing it at the panel as shown. Take care to curve the lines to run smoothly into the seam. Mark a balance mark across panel line below dart. Cut out the pattern and cut along panel line and along each side of dart. Outline pieces on fresh paper, add seam and hem allowances. Mark CF FOLD; label pattern pieces correctly. To find correct SG direction on side panel crease paper folding waist and hem edges midway. Cut waistband.

Making up

1. Stitch front panel seams, inserting pockets if appropriate. Press.
2. Stitch CB seams, insert zipper. Press.
3. Stitch side seams. Press.
4. Attach waistband and fastening.
5. Turn up and finish hem. Press.

Notes

1. You will have realised that because the dart has been transferred into the seam the fit of the skirt block has not been affected.

2. The straight skirt block could also be used for a panel design but it has two darts in the back so transfer one of them to the panel seam and leave the outer one to be stitched as a dart.

3. Another alternative which provides a style feature is to put only half the dart width into the front panel seam and dispose of the remainder by gathering the side panel. If you do this retain the back darts for a more stylish skirt.

4. If you habitually wear skirts with pleats it would be worth making a permanent copy of the panel skirt because it is a useful pattern for adding pleats. See below.

CB or side. If you wish to have a panel in the back, adapt it in the same way as for the front. The zipper could then be in the side or in the left panel seam. Another alternative is to put the zipper in the front left panel seam.

Back: Outline block, add seam and hem allowance, cut out.

(c) A-LINE SKIRT WITH SMALL PANEL PLEATS

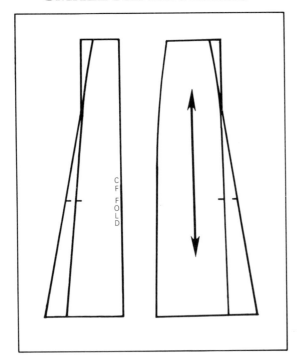

This style has a small pleat inserted in the panel seams at front and back if required. The zipper can be in the side or CB. This pleat is not supported at the waist so do not use it in soft fabrics or those with give, such as knits, as the pleats may drop below the hem.

Back: Outline A-Line block, add seam and hem allowances. Alternatively adapt to panel style and add pleats if required.

Front: Adapt front of A-Line block to panel style as described under (a) above. Cut out the panel pieces and outline on fresh paper. Add a wedge-shape to the panel edges 5cm (2in) wide at hem and tapering to nothing at the point where the panel curves to include the dart. Mark pleat depth point where extension is 2cm ($\frac{3}{4}$in) wide. Mark CF FOLD in centre panel; mark grain line in middle of side panel; transfer balance mark from panel seam to pleat edges. Add seam and hem allowances and cut pattern pieces folding the pleat exten-

sion back first in order to obtain the correct hemline. Cut waistband.

Making up

1. Stitch pleats from stitch point to waist. Stitch outer edges of pleat together. Press pleats towards centre.
2. Stitch CB seam or pleats.
3. Stitch side seams. Insert zipper.
4. Attach waistband and fastening.
5. Turn up and stitch hem.

Note

An alternative method of treating the hem with narrow pleats such as these is to omit the stitching joining the pleat edges together, turn up the hem, stitching the centre panel section separately. Place pleat edges together and stitch from hem edge up to top of pleat.

(d) PANEL SKIRT WITH INVERTED PLEATS

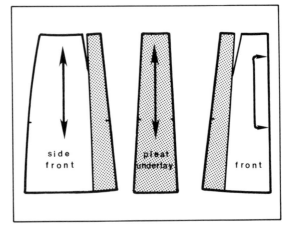

The illustration shows a mini or sports skirt which involves shortening the pattern but the same principles of adaptation apply to a skirt of any length. There are two inverted pleats with separate pleat backings in the front panel providing lots of room; the back may be plain A-Line with the zipper in the seam or it can be panelled with pleats inserted to balance the front. A seam pocket can be inserted in the right side seam if desired.

Back: Outline back A-Line block, shortening to desired length, add seam and hem allowance. Cut out.

Front: Outline front block, shortening to desired length, draw a straight panel line from the middle of the dart at the waist down to a point on the hemline about one third of the way along the hem from the CF edge. Cut out the pieces, place on fresh paper and add extension for pleat as follows: extend the hem edge on CF panel by 8cm (3¼in) and the waist by 6cm (2½in), rule a line between the two points. Transfer the panel balance mark to the pleat edge. At the waist, redraw the remaining side of the dart so that it curves gently into the pleat stitch line. Repeat on side panel. Mark CF FOLD on centre panel, SG on side panel. Add seam and hem allowances but do not cut round the pieces.

To cut the pleat backing fold a square piece of paper placing it against the centre panel and measure from the fold 6cm (2½in), mark this point level with the waist. With the fold still beside the centre panel measure out 8cm (3¼in) at hem level. Rule lines at top, bottom and vertically to join these points. Place against centre panel and transfer balance mark to both edges of the paper. Open out the pleat backing, rule straight grain along the crease and mark it CUT 2; add seam and hem allowances but do not cut out.

On centre and side panels fold under pleat extensions, place both pieces on the pleat backing, folds meeting along centre line of backing, pin together and cut out round all pattern pieces. This will produce the correct shape at hem and waist. Cut waistband.

Notes

If short of fabric or if it is bulky pleat backing need not extend right up to waist. Pleat backing may be made in contrast fabric.

Making up

1. Stitch side panels to centre panel RS together using a regular straight stitch from pleat point to waist and a large stitch from pleat point to hem which is removed later. press pleats open.

2. Place pleat underlay RS down on back of pleat, stitch pleat edges together from hem to waist.

3. Stitch CB seam and darts and insert zipper or construct pleats as for front.

4. Side seams; seam pocket if desired.

5. Waistband and fastening.

6. Turn up and stitch hem.

Notes

1. Light Fold-a-Band / Fuse'n'Fold / Waist-Shaper can be pressed to the back of the pleat folds but is probably not necessary in a sports or school skirt.

2. The alternative hem method described under design (b) can be used ie., stitching pleat backings to within 15cm (6in) of the hem, completing skirt, including the hem, and finally joining the remainder of the pleat backing.

3. Inverted pleats from the waist hang better if any topstitching is worked through skirt only before underlay is attached. An alternative decoration is to work arrowheads using buttonhole twist or thick thread such as Heavy Duty or Anchor Pearl.

4. If pleat backing does not extend to waist be sure to stitch horizontally through backing and pleat extension at top of pleat to ensure it does not drop in wear.

Skirts with Flare

The A-Line, or even straight, skirt block can be adapted to make flared skirts and if you have ever tried to do this just by adding extra to the side seams you will have realised it is not so simple if you want it to hang correctly. The additional fullness should be evenly distributed and the new SG position is important. Another principle to note is that the waist darts are dispensed with: the fuller the hemline the more curved becomes the waistline. Also it is important to insert the same amount of flare on both back and front skirt.

(a) SKIRT WITH SLIGHT FLARE

This adaptation will produce flare which begins at the hipline and gradually increases towards the hem. Back and front are cut to the fold.

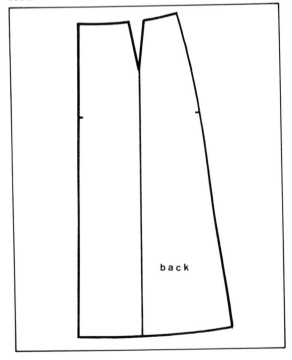

Back: Outline A-Line skirt block. Rule a vertical line from bottom of dart to hem, parallel with CB. Cut on this line from hem to base of dart. At waist fold over the dart: the pattern will open out below the dart. Place on new paper. Add extra to side seam, 2.5cm (1in) at hem and tapering to meet side seam at hip level. Outline the pattern, add seam and small hem allowance, mark CB FOLD and cut out.

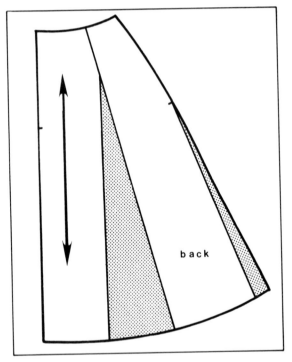

Front: Outline front A-Line block. Rule a line from dart point to hem parallel with CF and another midway between this line and CF. Cut along first line to dart point, fold dart to allow lower part to open out. Return to stage two of back pattern and measure the amount the pattern opened at the hemline. Measure the front at the same point and calculate the difference. Insert this amount in the front by cutting on the second line from hem to waist and overlapping at the waist until hem opens sufficiently. Pin to new paper, add 2.5cm (1in) at side edge as for back. Outline pattern, add seam and small hem allowance, mark CF FOLD and cut. Cut waistband.

Making up

1. On soft fabrics such as crepe or jersey insert a row of large machine stitching along waist 1cm ($\frac{3}{8}$in) from edge that can be eased up if necessary to make skirt fit waistband.

2. Side seams. Insert zipper in left seam. Press.

3. Attach waistband and fastening.

4. Turn up and stitch hem. Press.

(b) SKIRT WITH MODERATE FLARE

You will by now have grasped one of the basic principles of pattern drafting and in this and the next design you will begin to realise what pleasure there is in it.

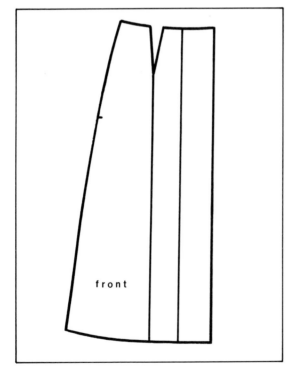

The sketch shows a skirt with a moderate amount of flare, suitable for medium weight fabrics, and with the waist darts incorporated in the waist shaping. There is a seam at CB and CF.

Back: Outline A-Line skirt block. Rule a line from base of dart to hem parallel with CB. Rule another line midway between that and CB and a third the same distance away on the far side of the dart. Cut along the central line to dart point and fold dart so that pattern

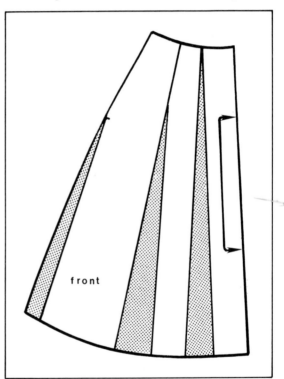

opens out below it. Place on fresh paper. cut on the other two lines from hem to waist and open the pieces until an amount equal to the first is inserted in the hemline. At side edge add half the amount that has been added in the other sections. Outline the new pattern. Add seam and hem allowances, mark CB edge and cut out making sure waist and hem are smooth curves. Find SG position by folding pattern with CB and side seams together. Open out and mark SG on crease.

Front: Outline front skirt block and adapt as for the back but, in the same way as for design (a) make sure the total flare added equals that already added to the back. Cut waistband.

Making up

1. Insert line of large stitches 1cm ($\frac{3}{8}$in) below waist edges to be eased up if necessary to make skirt fit waistband.
   2. Side seams; insert zipper in left seam.
   3. Waistband and fastening.
   4. Hem.

(c) FULLY FLARED SKIRT

For an even fuller skirt for soft fabrics the back and front A-Line blocks can have four vertical lines ruled on them, to be cut and spread exactly as explained under design (b) remembering to insert equal amounts back and front and half of one insertion at the side seam. If you wish you can keep cutting and spreading until the side seam edge is almost at right

angles to the CB or CF. In fact when it is at right angles you have a pattern for a quarter of a circular skirt but it is probably quicker to follow instructions on page 40 as this describes the method of marking the shape directly onto the fabric.

Making Up

Follow instructions for design (b).

(d) FOUR GORE SKIRT

Any flared skirt without darts can be made with a fold at CB and CF, the SG will therefore be at that point. Although the fabric design may demand that it is cut like that these skirts usually hang better with the SG centrally on each of four panels or gores, so entailing a seam at CB and CF. For designs such as stripes and checks that need matching it is essential to cut the skirt that way. Ensure that the stripes match by tracing them onto the pattern pieces, making sure they are drawn at the

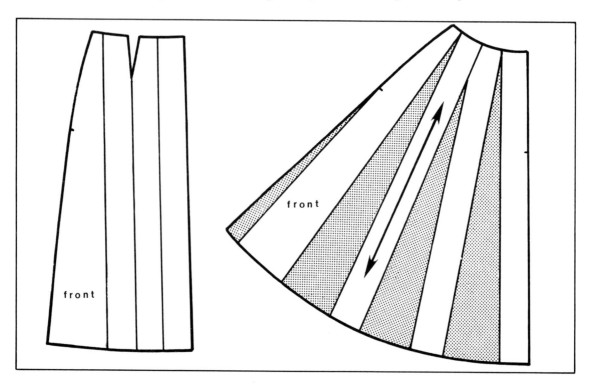

same level at matching seam edges, then they will match perfectly when sewn.

Making up
Follow instructions for design (b), starting by joining CF and CB seams.

(e) BIAS-CUT SKIRTS

In soft fabrics a bias skirt of any length from mini to floor can look very attractive. It is a useful style for underwear and nightwear as well as day and evening clothes.

Make the pattern to the desired fullness as described under design (b) or (c) with seams at CB and CF. Find SG position by folding pattern with both edges together; then fold again at right angles, crease both folds. Open out the pattern and rule a line to bisect the angle made by the creases. Cut waistband. Allow only narrow hems on bias skirts.

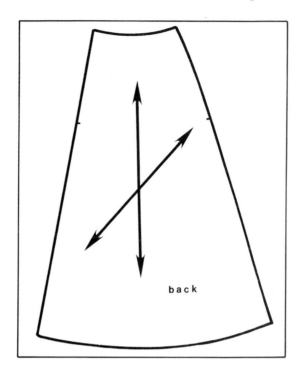

back

Wrap-over Skirt

The wrap can be at back or front, extending as far as required. Use straight or A-Line block; if using the straight block make sure the wrap is adequate.

The illustration shows a front-wrap style.

Back: Outline block; add seam and hem allowance; cut out.

Front: Outline block then reverse it and with CF edge on the CF line, outline again. Rule a line on the left skirt to indicate wrap; it should be angled outwards otherwise skirt will appear to be pulling open when worn. Hem corner could be curved. If you are unsure of the best position rule along inner edge of dart to two thirds of the way along the hem. Cut out the pattern, add an extension 3cm (1$\frac{1}{4}$in) wide to the front edge to make a turn-back facing wide enough to have light Fold-a-Band/

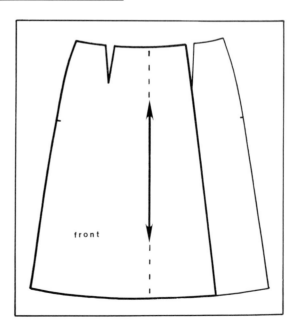

front

Fuse'n'Fold/Waist-Shaper attached. Mark SG along CF line. Mark skirt CUT 2. Add seam and hem allowances and cut out. Cut waistband.

Notes

1. The front could be gathered into the waistband instead of having darts. In this case draw the wrap line beyond the dart to allow more for gathering.

2. In lightweight fabrics a narrow hem only could be added along wrap edge and round skirt hem.

3. To make a flared wrap skirt, adapt the pattern to the required flare, cutting a whole front, then follow instructions above.

4. Remember to make the waistband the correct length.

Making up

1. Press Fold-a-Band/Fuse'n'Fold/Waist Shaper to WS wrap edge of right front if appropriate; neaten edge. Press facing to WS.

2. Stitch narrow hem along edge of left front.

3. Side seams.

4. Darts (or gathers).

5. Waistband and fastening.

6. With fold-back facing extended, turn up and stitch hem. Fold facing back into position on WS, loop stitch and slip stitch across facing and along lower edge of hem. Press.

7. Attach two or three Velcro 'Spot-ons' spaced between waist and thigh level to hold wrap closed.

Yoked Skirts

The yoke can be curved or pointed, shallow or deep but it should not extend below hip level. If you want the yoke below this level it is the lower part of the skirt that should be cut off and pleated or gathered, the upper part retaining the fit ie., darts etc., of the skirt block.

The principle behind cutting a pattern with a yoke is to transfer the darts from the waist to the horizontal yoke seam. Placing the shaping in this seam gives a good shape to the skirt and swing to the lower part.

(a) A-LINE YOKED SKIRT

The illustration shows a V-yoke, back centre seam CF zipper and belt loops on the waistband. The shape of the yoke can be varied as can the seaming and position of the zipper. Use either the straight or A-Line block depending on the shape required.

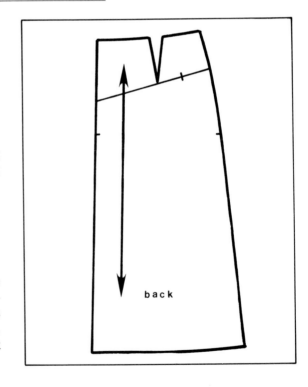

back

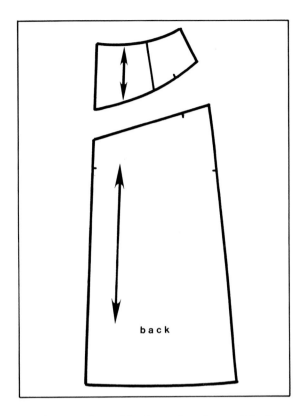

Back: Outline block; rule along SG line. Draw the yoke line slightly curved, to touch the point of the dart. Mark balance marks across the line. Cut out the pattern, cutting along yoke line. Fold the dart in the yoke, place on fresh paper and outline. Add seam allowance all round. Outline lower skirt section, add seam and hem allowance. Mark SG on both pieces.

Front: Outline block; rule long SG line. Draw yoke to desired shape making sure depth at side is the same as on the back. Fold out the dart, smoothing the paper flat below it. Place on fresh paper and outline. Add seam allowances. Cut out. Place lower section on fresh paper; add seam and hem allowance. Mark SG. Cut out. Cut waistband.

Making up

1. Stitch CB yoke seam. Join front yoke to back yoke at side seams. Make belt loops and stitch to RS at waist edge.

2. Stitch CB seam in lower skirt. Join side seams.

3. Attach yoke to skirt, matching seams.

4. Stitch CF seam to zipper point.

5. Insert zipper.

6. Attach waistband and fastening.

7. Turn up hem and stitch.

Note

If you wish to insert the zipper with a wide fly facing, add a wider seam allowance at CF of yoke and lower skirt.

(b) GATHERED YOKED SKIRT

With this type of design the darts are still transferred into the horizontal seam and fullness is inserted in the lower skirt. The zipper is at CB.

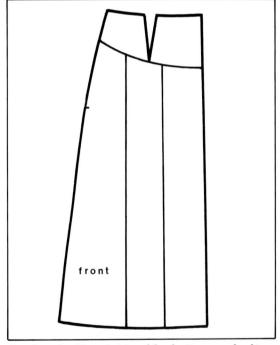

Back: Outline A-Line block. Draw yoke line. Make two balance marks across line. On lower skirt rule two vertical lines. Cut round outline and round yoke. Fold out dart, flattening paper to opposite edge. Place on fresh paper and outline. Add seam allowance all round.

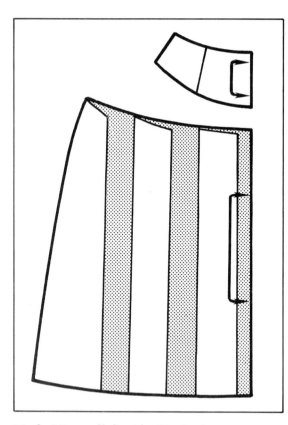

Mark SG parallel with CB. On lower section cut on lines and spread the pieces. Also add extra on CB edge. The total amount inserted should equal about half the original hem width of the back skirt block. Place on fresh paper and outline, drawing a smooth curve at waist and hem. Mark SG parallel with CB. Cut waistband.

Note

If you wish to make yoke double or lined mark it CUT 2.

Making up

1. Join front yoke to back yokes at side seams.

2. Stitch CB seam of lower skirt to zipper point.

3. Stitch and press side seams.

4. Gather lower skirt and attach yoke, matching seams.

5. Insert zipper in CB seam.

6. Attach waistband and fastening.

7. Turn up hem. Press.

Notes

1. Lower skirt could have unpressed pleats instead of gathers.

2. Zipper could be in left side if preferred and back skirt could be cut to a fold.

3. This style of skirt is also attractive if the lower part is flared. To do this draw the vertical lines as described but spread the pieces in a fan shape, adding fullness only at hem edge keeping upper edge the same length.

Circular Skirts

These patterns are amongst the simplest of all to make. They do not involve using the block, and can easily be marked directly onto the fabric using tailor's chalk or dots made with fabric pen. However, if you think you will use it frequently, perhaps for a child's skating or dancing skirt or for evening dresses or, if you have a patterned fabric that needs matching or balancing, it would be worth making a paper pattern.

There are three main types of circular skirt: one uses a quarter circle and could have one seam but is more usually made in two pieces, each cut on the bias (use for slim underwear and nightwear); the second uses a half circle and usually has two seams; the third is a full circle and it may have two or four seams depending on the design on the fabric. An even fuller skirt would consist of one and a half, two or even more full circles. Whatever the fullness at the hemline, the total waist edge of the plain circular skirt must be exactly waist size. An attractive variation is a gathered circular skirt which is in fact easier to do because the waist edge does not have to be cut to an accurate size. To do this make the waist of the skirt one and a half times as big as waist size and gather it to fit the waistband.

Pattern: Illustration shows one quarter of a full circular skirt. It is only necessary to make one piece of pattern. If marking directly onto fabric, draw and cut one quarter, then use that as the pattern for cutting three more. Rule two lines at right angles or use corner of paper or fabric.

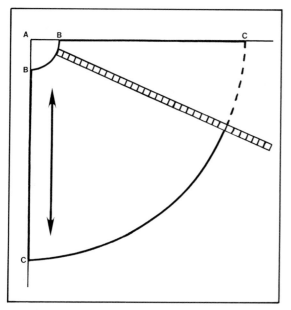

Beginning at point A measure $\frac{1}{6}$ waist measurement along both lines to points B. (The measurement along both lines is 10.5cm ($4\frac{1}{4}$) for a 63cm (25in) waist size.) If you have a compass draw the quarter circle. If not take the same measurement repeatedly from the corner and complete the circle freehand. Check the length of the arc and make sure it equals no more than $\frac{1}{4}$ the waist for a plain skirt. Seam allowances will be taken off but the edge is bound to stretch which will allow for this. Using a metre rule or tape measure

measure required skirt length plus $\frac{1}{6}$ waist measurement, 1cm ($\frac{3}{8}$in) hem allowance from A to C in both directions, then repeatedly until an arc is outlined. Add seam allowance at waist; mark SG and CB and CF FOLD on one edge. Mark pattern $\frac{1}{4}$ CIRCLE. Cut out. Cut waistband.

Notes

1. For a quarter circle skirt the waist curve must be equal to the waist measurement; for a half circle it must be half the waist measurement. You might find it useful to mark all three waistlines and hemlines carefully labelled, on one piece to make a master pattern to be traced each time you need one of the three designs.

2. The pattern can be made with four seams and not marked FOLD as above.

3. For a gathered circular skirt the arc at the waist must be approximately one and a half times bigger, or even more for fine fabrics.

4. Open fabric single to cut out.

5. If the full quarter circle will not fit onto your fabric, cut out as much as possible, use the spare fabric to seam a piece on where needed, joining selvedge to selvedge to maintain grain in pattern direction. Press seams open, replace pattern and cut remainder of hemline.

Making up

1. Stitch all seams leaving zipper opening at top of left side or CB seam.

2. Insert zipper.

3. Attach waistband and fastening.

4. Measure hem level. Turn and stitch narrow hem. Press.

Notes

1. Circular skirts always drop midway round each quarter where the fabric is on the bias. Cut out the pieces; pin to the rail of a coathanger and leave to hang for up to 4 days to allow it to drop to the fullest extent.

2. Unyielding fabrics may need to be snipped at waist edge when attaching waistband.

3. For gathered skirt insert gathering threads in each quarter before joining pieces.

4. A circular skirt hangs beautifully if the side seams are about 2.5cm (1in) towards the front of the body. This would entail making a back pattern with a waist arc 5cm (2in) bigger, ie., $\frac{1}{4}$ of that amount added to previous measurements. This in turn means that the front skirt waist arc must be shorter by the same amount. After you have made one pattern and understand the principle you should be able to work this out successfully.

Gathered or Dirndl Skirts

These are made from straight pieces of fabric without the use of the block or the need to make a pattern. For this reason it is one of the best garments for beginners to make and also because it is easy to construct. It is also the most successful way of using border fabrics ie., those that have a woven or printed design along one selvedge or that are shaded or one of the many scalloped-edge lace fabrics or broderie anglais. With these the border forms the hemline so the skirt can be made with only one seam and to calculate the amount of fabric required you need to know the width around the hemline. This can always be taken from an existing garment. The weight and bulk of the proposed fabric will govern the amount of fabric put into a gathered skirt. Generally a skirt in a fabric such as chiffon will not look good if it is not very full, unless perhaps it has full frills, ruffles or tiers added. A gathered skirt in heavy wool is enlarging to the figure but folded into unpressed pleats and made mid-calf it could be flattering to a lot of people.

Calculate the amount of fabric by assessing the number of widths you will use. It is not difficult to do this in the shop, gathering and bunching a width of material and holding it against you to see the effect. Full length skirts can be fuller than short ones because the length counteracts the width. One width of 150cm (54in) thick wool fabric would be sufficient; you would therefore add an amount for seam and hem plus waistband to your length and buy that amount. One width of 150cm (54in) fine wool crepe however, would hang fairly straight and you may want to use $1\frac{1}{2}$ widths. Two widths, ie., twice your length plus allowances, of 90cm (36in) fabric is ample for a short cotton skirt, in fact you could even reduce it a little by taking the waistband along one selvedge. If you are using lawn or voile or georgette however, three or even four widths could be used, especially for a long skirt. Use $1\frac{1}{2}$ widths of fabric 115cm (45in) wide. This will leave plenty of fabric for the waistband and would even waste a piece so plan a design with big patch pockets, tie-round sash, a rouleau tubing tie to thread through loops on the waistband, a headscarf, straps or braces, or some such feature, to use it up.

Cutting out

Cut across the fabric on the straight grain to make two pieces. Cut waistband. With one-way designs turn one piece round before joining seams so design goes in the same direction on back and front. If using a border fabric decide which part of the border is most suitable for the hem edge of the skirt, turn up and press a crease along the length of fabric. Cut across the width to straighten the ends if necessary. Measure your length plus 1.5cm ($\frac{5}{8}$in) from the fold and cut along the length of fabric. Cut waistband, pockets etc., from the strip you have cut off.

Making up

1. Stitch seams; press. If seams wrinkle snip selvedges. Another remedy is to cut narrow strips of Wundaweb/Stitch Witchery/Save-a-Stitch and slip them between the seam allowance and garment; press with seam pulled out taut and pinned to ironing board.

2. Insert zipper. This may be at CB or side although if skirt has only one seam it is usually at CB.

3. Insert gathering threads only along waist edge. Measure skirt length from waist, turn up and press hem evenly all round skirt. Stitch hem or trim depth to 3cm (1¼in) and insert Wundaweb/Stitch Witchery/Save-a-Stitch. Press.

4. Gather waist; attach waistband and fasteners.

Notes

1. The gathers can be arranged to suit the figure ie., less at sides.

2. Fabric can be formed into unpressed pleats instead of gathers. You could arrange them so that one overlaps the zipper opening and so dispense with the zipper in a full skirt. The opening should not be at CB in this case.

3. The smoothest waist of all is achieved by making several large unpressed pleats and then gathering across them right round the skirt. Another way of reducing bulk at the waist is to make a few very long darts before gathering.

4. There are a number of decorative additions that are possible including frills or ruffles, tucks, edgings, bands, underlayers etc., and fabrics such as Tana lawn in particular look delightful if two contrasting skirts of different lengths are gathered into one waistband. If you are designing a skirt with additions be sure to work out the precise length of each piece, subtracting frills or ruffles from total length for example, and calculate your fabric accurately. Frills or ruffles can be single or double, attached to the bottom or applied above the hem and should be at least 1½ times the width of the skirt.

5. Any of the waistbands described on page 110ff. can be used, including particularly the one that uses elastic. Shaped waistbands can also be designed. Draw the shape you require – curved, heart-shape etc., on a piece of folded paper, the fold representing CF, curve the lower edge slightly and allow a long overlap for fastening. Cut out and fit; adjust and re-shape. Cut the exact size required in Heavy Pelmet weight Vilene/Pellon then cut two pieces of fabric for it adding seam allowances. A thin layer of wadding can be inserted under outer layer of fabric. Fasten waistband with at least 6cm (2½in) Velcro. 6. If you have a hollow back or other waist fitting problem remember that the same adjustment needs to be made to a gathered skirt. After joining seams and before inserting zipper, fold skirt along CF and CB and shape waist edge as appropriate.

6. For a dress with a gathered skirt follow the instructions for cutting but joining skirt to bodice at appropriate stage.

Tiered Skirts

This is a variation of a gathered skirt. Its advantages are that it can be full at hem level but have minimum bulk at the waist and it can be made out of less fabric, even remnants. A short skirt can consist of three or even two tiers, a full length skirt would have three or four. For best effect vary the depth of each tier with the deepest at the bottom. The following is a guide: For a skirt 70cm (27in) long make the top tier 19cm ($7\frac{1}{2}$in), the middle one 23cm (9in) and the bottom one 28cm (11in). These are finished measurements so cut out adding seam allowance, and hem allowance on the bottom one. Use 1 width of fabric for the top tier, $1\frac{1}{2}$ for the middle one and $2\frac{1}{2}$ for the bottom one, using 115cm (45in) wide fabric. This would take less than 2 metres ($2\frac{1}{4}$yds) of fabric and yet have a hem width of 280cm (110in).

Making up
1. Join up the $2\frac{1}{2}$ widths allowed for bottom tier, press seams open.

2. Turn up and press hem. Stitch or trim to 3cm ($1\frac{1}{4}$in) and hold with Wundaweb/Stitch Witchery/Save-a-Stitch. Press. Fold into 4 and press the creases at the raw edge. Insert a gathering thread in each quarter 1cm ($\frac{3}{8}$in) inside the raw edge.

3. Join up the ends of the $1\frac{1}{2}$ widths cut for the middle tier leaving 4cm ($1\frac{1}{2}$in) open at the top of one of the seams for the zipper. Press seams open.

4. Divide into 4 and press creases. Join lower tier to middle tier, pulling up gathers to fit.

5. Insert gathering threads in each quarter along upper edge 1cm ($\frac{3}{8}$in) within the edge. Join to upper tier, match zipper edges to ends of upper tier. Insert zipper.

6. Insert a gathering thread along upper edge of skirt. Attach waistband with fastenings. Press.

FRILLS OR RUFFLES

Frills or ruffles of self fabric, contrast, lace, pre-gathered edgings etc., can be added to flared or gathered skirts, even to an A-Line skirt or with certain designs to a straight skirt. Calculate the most suitable depth for the skirt, add a seam allowance for the upper edge or a hem allowance if it is placed on the RS of the skirt to give the upper edge a frill or ruffle too; add a hem allowance for the lower edge. As the frill or ruffle will weight the skirt the hem can be narrow, perhaps rolled with the hemming foot, or 3cm ($1\frac{1}{4}$in) wide to take Wundaweb/Stitch Witchery/Save-a-Stitch. Allow for $1\frac{1}{2}$ times the width of the skirt at the point it will be attached for gathering. If the frill or ruffle is to be narrow consider making it double with the fold at the bottom. It is much easier to make, is crisp and adds weight to the skirt.

If the frill or ruffle is to be gathered on top of the skirt with both hems level, you will need to add the amount for the frill or ruffle to the fabric required for the skirt. If the frill or ruffle is to replace a portion of the skirt, make the skirt pattern, then measure the frill or ruffle depth up from the hemline at intervals. Cut off the lower piece, add seam allowances to skirt pattern and cut. It is not necessary to cut paper patterns for the frill or ruffle pieces as they are simply straight pieces of fabric but for future use make a note on the pieces of skirt pattern of exactly what the measurements of the frill or ruffle pieces are.

Making up
For a frill or ruffle to be applied to the skirt:
1. Join frill or ruffle ends and press. Hem upper and lower edges; press into 4 and insert gathering threads in each quarter.

2. Mark a line on the finished skirt at the correct depth; divide skirt into 4 at that level.

Pin the frill or ruffle to the skirt, pull up gathers to fit and attach by working a zig-zag stitch over the gathering thread.

For a frill or ruffle attached to the bottom of the skirt:

1. Join the skirt seams. Insert zipper, attach waistband and fastening.

2. Join ends of frill or ruffle. Press. Hem lower edge of frill or ruffle. Fold into 4 and press. Insert a gathering thread in each quarter.

3. Divide lower edge of skirt into 4. Place frill or ruffle RS down to RS skirt, matching quarters and pin. Pull up gathers to fit. Stitch and neaten. Press.

Tucks

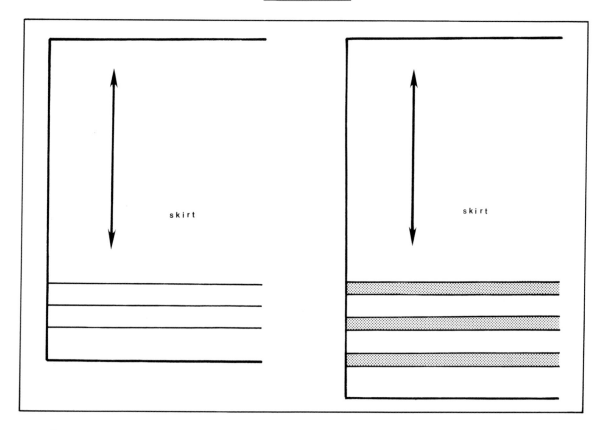

A gathered skirt can have a series of even or graduated tucks above the hem. In addition to being decorative they add weight. Decide on the depth of tuck required, allow twice that amount for each tuck on each width of fabric to be used and add that amount to the quantity of skirt fabric. On the pattern mark the position of each tuck – they need not be evenly spaced – and cut the pattern on the lines. Either spread out the pieces on fresh paper and outline a new pattern or, a better idea is to spread out the pieces of pattern directly on the fabric, allowing space for the tucks. After cutting out, the tuck positions can be marked with tailor tacks beside the cut edges of the paper.

Making up

1. Stitch and press skirt seams.
2. Insert zipper. Attach waistband and fastenings.

3. Turn up and finish skirt hem.
4. Fold skirt WS together along first tuck position, press and stitch. Repeat for remaining tucks checking finished length of skirt. Press.

Pleats All Round

These skirts can be made without making a pattern; this includes kilts. The pleats are made to fit at hip level which is where they hang from, they are overlapped above that until the fabric is reduced to waist size.

hip measurement, more if pleats are to be left unstitched. Allow three times this width of fabric for pleating. Cut straight pieces of fabric to length plus seam and hem allowance and join up leaving one seam open.

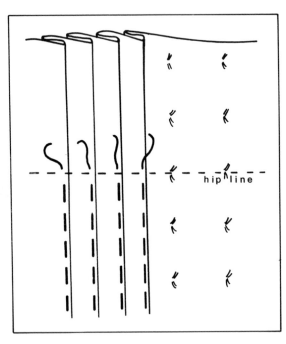

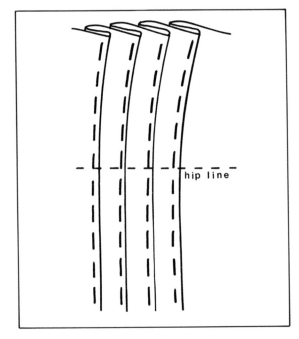

KNIFE PLEATS

The pleats may be stitched down to hip level or left pressed. Add 3cm (1¼in) ease to your

Making up

1. Experiment to see what depth of pleat works best in the fabric. If it is striped or check use the lines for folding. If it is plain

mark out the pleat positions with tailor tacks or chalk.

2. Measure your hip depth down from waist edge and fold over and pin the pleats at that level. Pin for a quarter of the skirt and check the measurement. When correct fold and baste all pleats from hip level to hem. Press well.

3. Above hip level fold each pleat over a little further at the waist and baste from waist to hip level. Once more check after doing a quarter to make sure the size is correct. Press well. Stitch if required.

4. Join remaining seam.

5. Insert zipper.

6. Attach waistband and fastenings.

7. Remove some basting from hemline, turn up hem and stitch. Refold and re-baste pleats. Press well. Remove all bastes.

KILT

This is made on the same principle as the pleated skirt but allow a flat piece of about 20–25cm (8–10in) on each side of the pleats for the outer and inner front layers. Make up as described above but begin by hemming and fringing the edge of the outer wrap. Cut the waistband as for a wrap-over skirt.

Notes

1. If fabric is soft or loosely woven make a lining down to hip level using the straight skirt block.

2. On a kilt the backs of the pleats can be stabilised either with a piece of lining hemmed along the lower edge onto the backs of the pleats at hip level or hem a piece of tape at hip level.

3. It helps if you can turn up and finish the hem before folding in the pleats. This is easy enough with a kilt but less so with a skirt. If you do it, check the fit of the skirt after basting on the waistband but before stitching it. The skirt can be lifted or dropped at the waist to get the hem level.

4. Try to arrange that a pleat folds over the zipper for a neat finish. This usually means putting in an extra pleat.

5. Don't worry if the pleated fabric is slightly big; the surplus can be taken out of the final seam. With a kilt it can be cut off the end of the inner flat area.

6. A child's waist and hip measurements may be the same so the pleats will be folded straight from waist to hem. The skirt can be held up with straps or with elastic through the waistband.

TROUSER DESIGNS

Whatever style or length of trousers you decide on, try to make sure you do not alter the length or shape of the crotch seam so that your trousers continue to fit you. Extra width for baggy styles can be added but if you change size or shape dramatically it would be worth tracing off another size block from the master pattern, adjusting it as before to a well fitting block.

(a) TAPERED TROUSERS

Decide on required length ie., full length, above ankle, below knee etc. If necessary take a measurement along the inside leg seam of an existing pair of trousers. Outline front and back trouser block, rule a line across each leg at the required length. Decide on the width you want the leg at the hemline: below-knee trousers need to be loose enough to ride up when you bend your knees; full length tight trousers will often have to have a short slit in the outside leg seam partly to allow for movement, partly to make sure you can get your foot through. Measure total width of trouser block at new hem level and calculate the reduction that will be necessary. Divide the amount by 4 and mark off that distance on each seam of each leg. Draw smooth curves from new points back to original lines. Use your flexible curve if you have one. For below-knee trousers you can re-join the original seam as high as 5cm (2in) from crotch level if you want the trousers tight over the thighs as

well. Take care not to make them too tight. Remember that a reduction of as little as 1cm ($\frac{3}{8}$in) on one line means a total of 4cm ($1\frac{1}{2}$in) on that leg; run the tape measure round your thigh to check as you draw. Alter back and front alike; back only is illustrated. Trim off surplus paper, place pattern on fresh paper, outline and add seam and hem allowances. Add SG arrow. Cut waistband.

Note

If you want to make this style of trousers in stretch fabric such as Lycra, the reduction for fit will depend on the particular fabric so it is best to make the alteration above and rely on fitting for the remainder.

Making up

1. Stitch inside leg and outside leg seams. Press open.
2. Stitch and press darts.
3. Press creases if appropriate.
4. Join crotch seam from zipper point to back waist. Press open from back waist to start of crotch curve. Do not snip the seam allowances.
5. Insert zipper.
6. Attach waistband and fastening.
7. Turn up and stitch hems. Press.

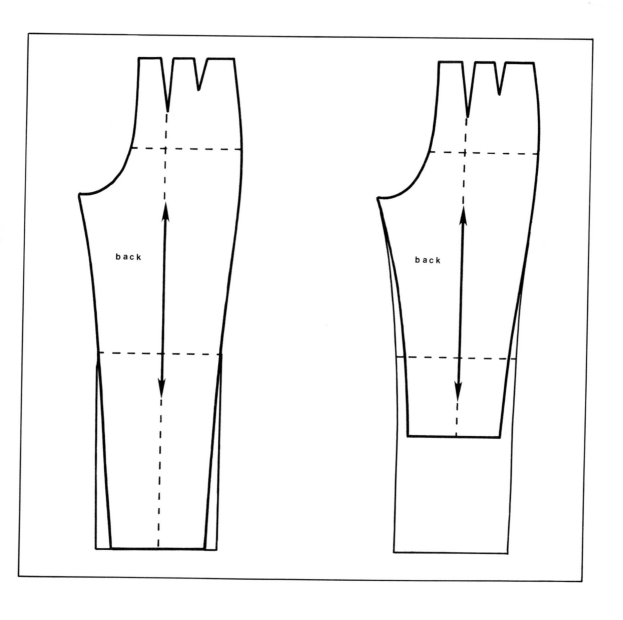

(b) FLARED TROUSERS

Decide on the amount of flare you require and also the length; full length trousers look better worn longer than straight or tapered styles. If you are unsure of a suitable hem width, measure some existing trousers. Also remember that if you are shorter than average height, curtail your enthusiasm and have only moderate flare. Also decide on the depth of flare required ie., whether it should start below the knee or above. At hem level add a quarter of the proposed increase on the outer

and inner leg seam on back and front. If the amount added to each seam is more than 4cm ($1\frac{1}{2}$in), add the remainder to the outside leg seam only. Taper new seam lines to meet original pattern either at knee level or 5cm (2in) from crotch level on inside leg and 5cm (2in) below hip level on outside leg. Smooth seam lines are very important; use your flexible curve. Draw curved hems as shown. Add seam and hem allowances. Cut waistband.

Making up
See (a) above.

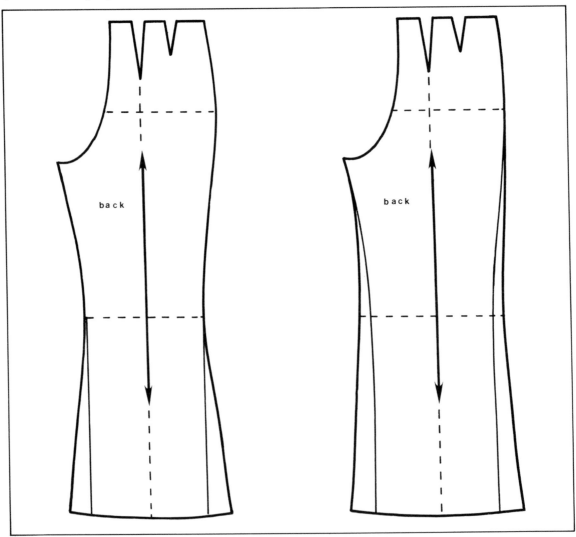

(c) TRACKSUIT TROUSERS

These are made with elastic in the waist and sufficient extra fullness at the waist to enable the zipper to be omitted. Ankle hems can have elastic or drawstrings.

Back: Outline straight-legged trouser block. Draw new CB and side seam lines vertically up from hip level. Add extra depth to allow for casing for elastic; allow twice the width of the elastic plus ease ie., for 2.5cm (1in) wide elastic add 6cm (2½in). Add on casing depth at trouser hem too. Add seam allowances all round and cut.

Front: Adapt as for back. Mark fold over line between top edge and waist. As the side edges are straight the trousers can be cut without side seams if the fabric is wide enough. To do

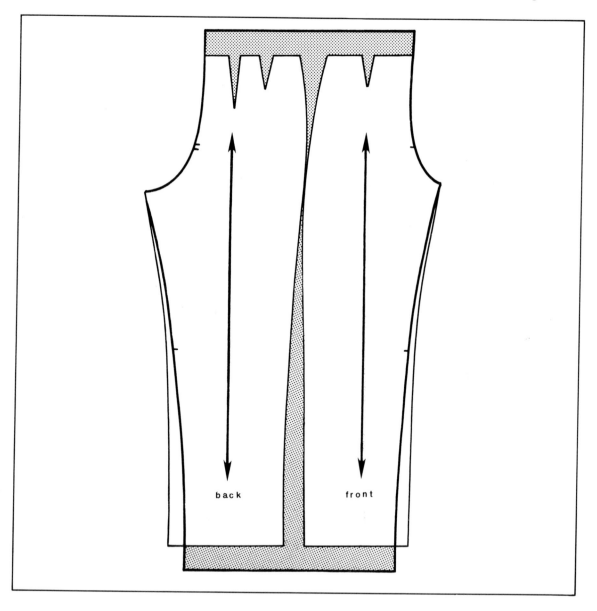

back   front

this, place both blocks on paper with hip lines touching and grain arrows parallel. Outline, adapt waist and hemline as above.

Making up

1. Stitch side seams and inside leg seams.
2. Join crotch seam.
3. Fold over casing at waist and hems and stitch. Insert elastic to fit.

Notes

1. An even deeper casing can be allowed so that two rows of stitching can be inserted to form twin channels for two narrower pieces of elastic. This is not only an attractive finish it is more comfortable to wear, with a less rigid grip than wide elastic. Allow four times width of elastic plus two amounts of ease.

2. Ankles can be left ungathered. If you do this, add on hem allowance only. The trousers could also be tapered and have slits or zippers inserted.

3. For more waist fullness cut block from waist to hem and spread out, inserting fullness at waist only, in addition to drawing straight seam edges.

4. When making up, neat elastic slots can

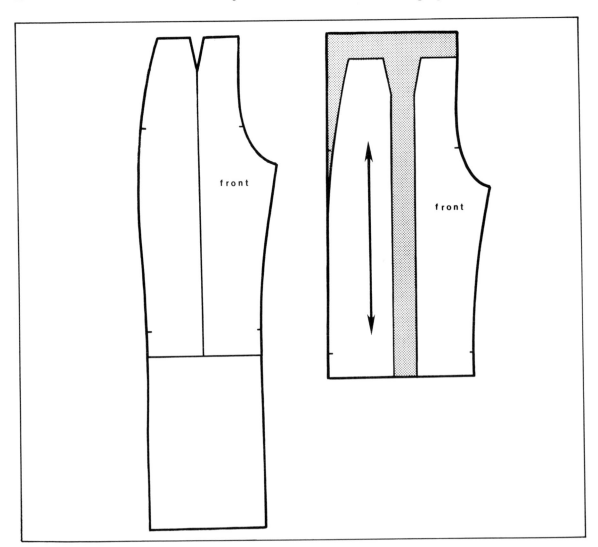

be made, leaving a gap for threading elastic by stopping the side seam stitching for a short distance 2cm ($\frac{3}{4}$in) below the waist edge.

(d) GATHERED TROUSERS

These are easy to make and fit but are not very flattering to any but tall slim figures. The illustration shows below-knee length trousers but they can be full length.

Back and front: Outline the straight leg block. Shorten if required. Rule a vertical line from the point of the dart to the hem, parallel with the grain line. Cut on this line and spread out the pattern pieces on fresh paper. The amount you insert should be $\frac{1}{4}$ of the total extra fullness you need on the total or $\frac{1}{2}$ the extra you want to insert in one leg. For full length evening trousers in a fabric such as chiffon you could insert as much as 40cm (16in), depending on the total width of the fabric being used. Outline the pattern; add seam and hem allowances. Cut a waistband pattern or, if preferred, add on an extension

for a casing for elastic as described under (c) above. Also, if the style demands you can add casings for elastic at the ankles.

Notes

1. If you make the trousers very full they become more like culottes and will therefore need a slightly lower crotch seam but this can be adjusted at fitting.

2. Seam pockets can be used; the outline is disguised by the gathers.

3. Insert the zipper in the side or CB seam.

Making up

1. Insert gathering threads along waist edge of all four pieces, ignoring the original darts.

2. Join fronts to backs and stitch inside leg seams and side seams.

3. Insert zipper in left seam.

4. Join crotch seam.

5. Gather waist and attach waistband.

6. Turn up and stitch hems.

(e) FRONT-PLEATED TROUSERS

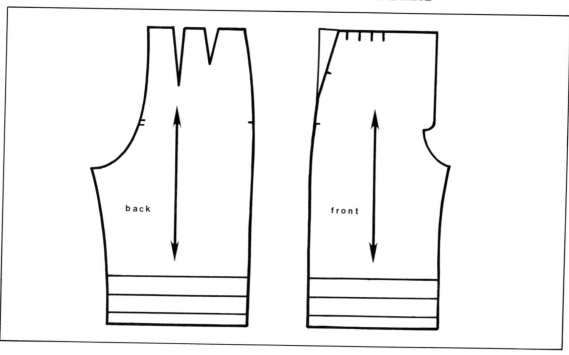

back

front

This style has four tucks in the front, a CF zipper and usually slanted, inset pockets. The illustration shows the trouser block shortened for Bermuda shorts and hem extensions for turn-ups but the waist alteration and addition of zipper extension is the same for any length.

Back: Outline block. Make any alteration required for length and width. Add seam and hem allowance.

Front: Outline block, make the same alterations to length etc., as for back. At waist add 4cm ($1\frac{1}{2}$in) to width at side seam. Draw a smooth line from there to join original side seam at hip level. The amount to be taken out in pleats is 4cm ($1\frac{1}{2}$in) plus the width of the dart. Divide this total into two and draw in two tucks, one at the dart position, the other 2.5cm (1in) further towards side seam. At CF draw a line parallel with CF edge 2.5cm (1in) from it for zipper extension, curving it to meet original line just below hip level. For slanted pockets follow instructions on page 107. Add seam and hem allowances, cut out. Cut waistband.

Making up

As for (a) but folding pleats at front instead of darts. Note that this style allows for last minute alterations in waist size which is useful.

(f) OXFORD BAGS

This term describes wide-legged pleated trousers with turn-ups. The illustration shows a pair with a front zipper. Inset slant pockets could also be added as in design (e) above.

Back: Outline straight block. Rule new vertical seam lines from knee level to hem. Above knee level, curve the new lines to meet the original line at thigh level and just below crotch level. Decide on required width of turn-up and add $2\frac{1}{2}$ times that much to the length. Rule a long SG line from hem to dart

point to act as a crease position. Add seam and hem allowances.

Front: Outline straight block. At side edge, rule a vertical line from hip level to waist. Divide this extra waist size plus the dart width into two and draw two waistline tucks. Add fly extension 2.5cm (1in) wide. Rule vertical lines from knee to hem adding slightly less to the inside leg at the hem than on the back. Curve the seam lines back to meet the originals at hip level and just below crotch. Add turn-up as for back. Draw crease line from point of original dart. Add seam and hem allowance. Cut waistband.

Making up

1. Stitch outside and inside leg seams. Press.
2. Stitch back darts.
3. Fold front pleats into position and stitch across the top to secure.
4. Press creases in both legs.
5. Stitch crotch seam to join legs.
6. Insert zipper.
7. Attach waistband and fastenings.
8. Turn up and stitch hems. Fold turn-ups into position, secure with bar tacks. Press well.

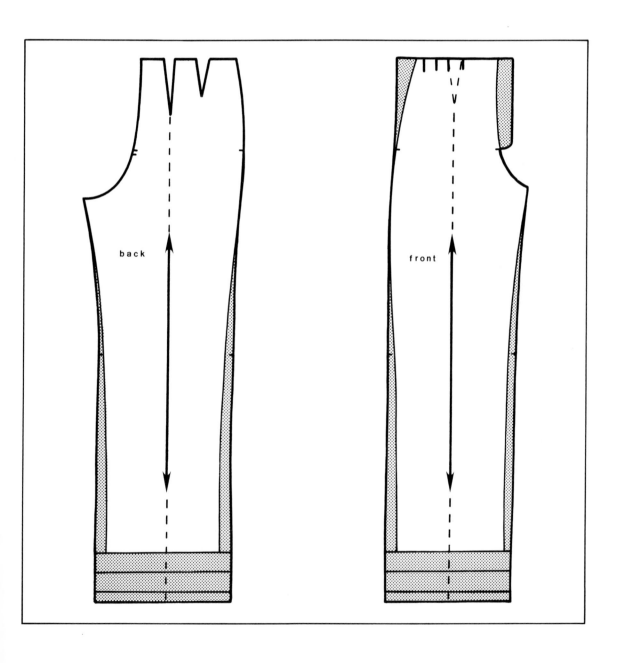

Shorts

Shorts of all lengths can be made by simply shortening the trouser block. The adaptation is so straightforward that once you have established a length for shorts the hemline could be drawn on the trouser block for future use.

(a) SHORT SHORTS

Back: Outline straight trouser block to thigh level. Rule a horizontal guide line at required hem level: this can be established by measuring the length on the inside leg seam. Shape the hemline by curving it down below the guide line by 1cm ($\frac{3}{8}$in). Add seam and hem allowance.

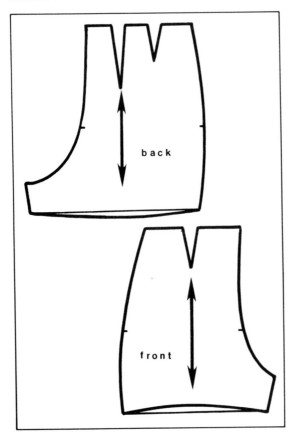

back

front

Front: Outline front trouser block and rule a hem guide line as on the front making sure that both side seam and inside leg seam edges are equal in length. Draw a curved hemline this time 1cm ($\frac{3}{8}$in) above the guide line. Cut waistband.

Notes

1. Front darts can be replaced by a tuck. Alternatively the adjustment for front pleats and zipper can be made as in trouser style (e).

2. The zipper can be in the front or left side of the shorts.

3. The hemline can be as narrow as 1.5cm ($\frac{5}{8}$in) for a narrow machined hem.

4. For elasticated waist adapt the waist edge and add a casing as for trousers (c).

5. Patch pockets, seam pockets and shaped inset pockets are suitable for shorts.

6. If you want to make hemline slits in the side seams, cut out shorts with 2.5cm (1in) side seam allowance.

Making up

1. Join the two front sections along crotch seam, inserting zipper in upper part if appropriate.

2. Join back crotch seam; press.

3. Insert all darts.

4. With back and front together join side seams. Insert zipper in left seam if appropriate.

5. Stitch underleg seam of shorts, matching front and back crotch seams. Press.

6. Turn up and stitch hems.

7. Attach waistband and fastening.

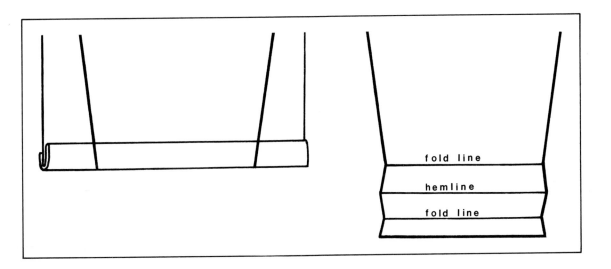

(b) BERMUDA SHORTS

These can be any length above the knee and made from the block using either the fitted leg or straight leg seam. The waist can be extended or pleated or have the usual darts. The zipper is normally at CF. The illustration shows Bermudas with turn-ups but the hems can be just straight, possibly with short slits in the side seams.

Back and front: Outline trouser block on straight or fitted leg as far as knee level. Decide on required length and draw hemline. Adjust waist shaping if necessary. Before cut-ting the pattern, fold the paper at the hemline to form a turn-up approximately 4cm (1½in), folding it onto RS, taking paper under to WS and trimming it off at half turning width. Mark seam lines across fold of turning using toothed tracing wheel and cut on the line through the folded paper. Open out the pattern and you will have the correct shaped seam. Add seam and hem allowances to pattern and cut. Cut waistband. Cut patch or seam pockets if required.

Making up
Follow order given for (f) Oxford bags.

Culottes

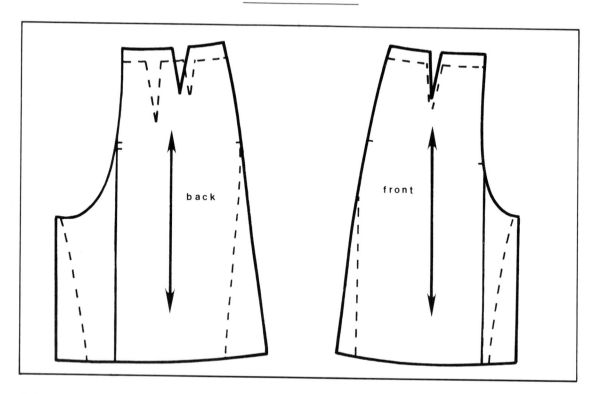

Culottes are wide-legged trousers with a loose fitting crotch. they can be any length. The waist can be darted or gathered into the waistband. You will need the A-Line skirt block as well as the trouser block to make culotte patterns.

(a) BASIC CULOTTES

These are plain with A-Line shape.

Back: Outline A-Line skirt block; adjust to length required for culottes. Place trouser block on top with grain lines parallel and CB edges together but have the waist of the trousers 2cm ($\frac{3}{4}$in) below the skirt waist. Outline the crotch seam. Extend crotch line by 1cm ($\frac{3}{8}$in) then draw a vertical line from there to hem level: the line must be parallel with the SG line. The remainder of the pattern, waist edge, dart, side seam and hem are as skirt block. Add seam and hem allowances.

Front: Outline A-Line skirt block, place trouser block on top and outline crotch seam exactly as for back. Add seam and hem allowance of suitable depth for a skirt. cut out pattern. Cut waistband.

Making up
1. Stitch and press outside leg and inside leg seams, inserting the zipper in left side seam.
2. Stitch darts.
3. Join legs; stitch crotch seam.
4. Attach waistband and fastening.
5. Turn up and stitch hems. Press.

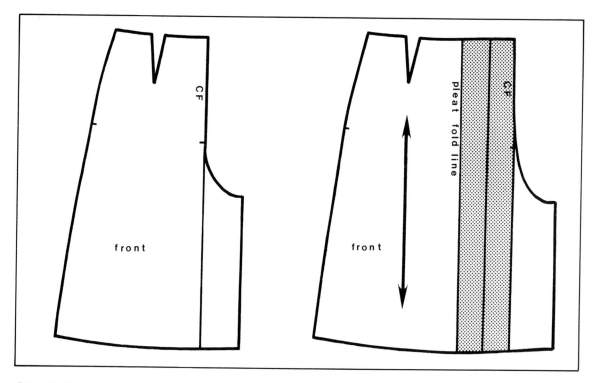

(b) PLEATED CULOTTES

These are more flattering to most figures as the CF and CB pleat conceals the crotch area. The pleats may be pressed and hang loose from the waist or they may be topstitched as far as hip level. The zipper is in the left side.

Back: Outline A-Line skirt pattern and crotch seam of trouser block as described for (a) Basic culottes. Cut along CB line, open out pattern pieces and insert 16cm (6¼in). Place on fresh paper and outline. Add seam and hem allowance.

Front: Make pattern as described for back. Cut waistband pattern.

Making up

1. Insert pleats. Make loose darts by bringing pleat line over to meet CF and CB lines. Baste and press.

2. Make up culottes as for (a) above, leave basting in place until you are ready to stitch the hems.

To make stitched pleats place the two front sections RS together and stitch along pleat line from waist to hip line with normal machine stitch and from hipline to hem with large stitch. Press pleat. Repeat with back culotte pieces. Continue making up following (a) above stitching outside and inside leg seams and then crotch seam. Remove large stitches in pleat when you are ready to stitch the hems.

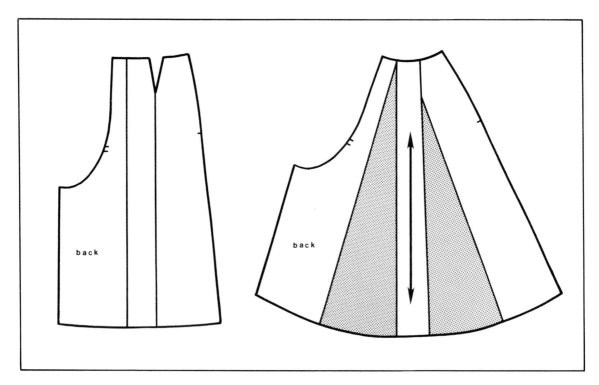

(c) FLARED CULOTTES

These are attractive in lightweight fabrics. They can be any length from mini-length for dancing and sports to ankle length. The amount of flare you add will depend on the type and width of the fabric.

Back: Outline A-Line skirt block and add crotch curve from trouser block as described for (a) above. Rule a line from point of dart to hem and another closer to the CB. Cut along both lines. Close up the dart and allow the hemline to open. Open the pattern on the second line and allow the same amount of flare at the hem. Outline on fresh paper. Add seam and hem allowance. Cut out. Find SG position by folding pattern in half at hemline and creasing.

Front: Cut front pattern as for back. Cut waistband.

Making up
Follow order given for (a) above.

BODICE DESIGNS
Bust Shaping

The shaping in all areas of garments is important but probably more so for the bust. This is not only so that the garment looks flattering and feels comfortable but because the piece of fabric is small and there is less space in which to gradually lessen the effect of the shaping. This makes accuracy more important. The truth of this point is proved by the fact that the bust shaping is easier to cope with if it comes from the shoulder where there is a greater distance to the opposite side of the piece of garment, creating more gradual fullness. This is a point to remember when fitting a large size bust.

The bodice block has two darts: one underarm and one at the waist. They are both directed towards the bust point. The waist dart has the dual function of reducing the waist as well as providing shape for the bust. Remember that it is often best to take in side seams in order to fit the waist more closely because a bigger dart also increases the bust shaping, which may not be needed. As with other parts of a garment, the dart must be directed towards the bulge of the body but because the bust is a more sudden, more compact, bulge than, say the bottom, it must stop short of the bust unless emphasis is required, for example, on a tight or strapless bodice. There must also be room for movement as well as ease for comfort and the larger the bust the less closely it should be fitted for comfort.

Large women often find darts restricting and prefer soft gathers for this reason.

Every bodice must have shaping for the bust and provided it has been allowed for at the pattern edge and it is directed towards the bust, it need not be kept where it is on the block. The bust shaping can be done from any of the outer edges of the pattern. Also, the shaping need not necessarily be stitched as a dart: the equivalent amount can be gathered or eased or divided into tucks. Also, the amount of shaping can be increased if you wish, to make more gathers etc. This is what designing is and the benefit of learning to do it yourself is that you can vary the position and amount of fullness to suit your figure and the fabric you are using.

It follows that the larger the bust the bigger the bust dart or equivalent shaping but this information can be used in other ways. If a small-busted or flat-chested person uses bust darts of the correct size for her and fits them closely, she will look even more flat-chested. She can gather or tuck the fabric instead, even increase the amount, as a disguise. This is another aspect of designing and another good reason for learning to do it yourself.

Before you go any further find out for yourself, with the following exercise, how easy and satisfying it is to move the bust shaping. Trace off the front bodice block and cut it out. Mark the underarm and waist darts, then re-

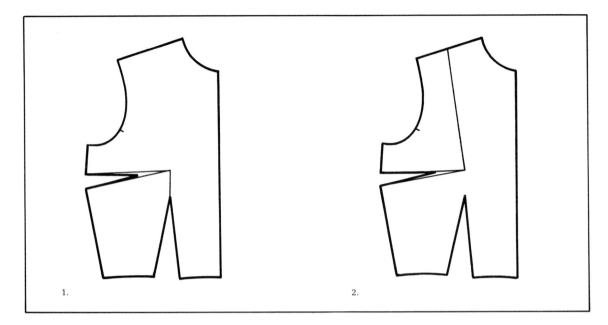

1.   2.

draw them as follows: Rule a vertical line up from the top of the waist dart. Re-draw the underarm dart so that the point meets the vertical line (1). Draw a line from mid-shoulder to meet at the same point (2). Where the lines meet is the Bust Point. Cut out the underarm and waist darts, and cut along the line from the shoulder but leave the paper joined at the Bust Point. Now try moving the pieces around keeping the CF still. First close the underarm dart and you will find all the shaping opening up at the waist (3). Next, close up the underarm and watch it appear in the shoulder (4). Although the edges are open wider at the pattern edge, the amount of shaping is the same: the V shape radiating from the Bust Point which will now be referred to as (BP), is exactly the same. You can now see why it is so important to spend time getting the bust dart to fit and how if you solve your fitting problems on the block, any style adaptation you make thereafter is for design purposes: your pattern will still fit.

As a further experiment and for future information, try folding out the dart, in any of the above positions, stopping short of BP. Also try folding it into two short tucks to see the effect

on you (5). Finally, divide the shaping by opening up two darts, shoulder and waist, shoulder and underarm etc. Small sizes can often use the shaping in one place but larger busts usually need a split, for comfort as well as appearance. Never plan for a dart to be stitched right to BP. The point of the dart should be 2–3cm ($\frac{3}{4}$–$1\frac{1}{4}$in) away, depending on figure size. You can see from the basic block that both darts stop short of BP.

Continue experimenting with the bust shaping, even cutting out fronts in fabric to try them on yourself or on a dummy. The following are some suggestions:

(a) Draw a line from BP sloping down to CF edge, cut on the line (6). Close underarm dart (7). Pattern is cut to a seam, both edges are gathered.

(b) Rule a line from BP to neckline edge; cut on the line (8). Close underarm dart (9). Gather and bind neckline; gather waist edge instead of stitching dart in place.

(c) Close underarm dart to transfer all shaping to waist edge and gather (3). If you made this into a pattern this could be the bodice of a dress with drawstring or elastic waist.

(d) Rule a line from half-way down armhole to

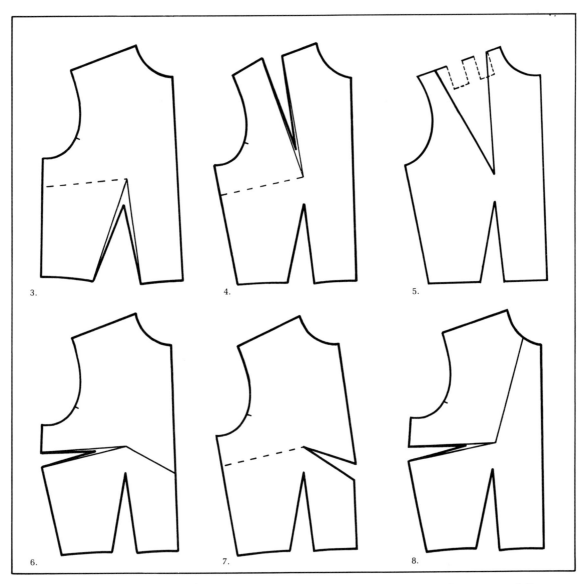

BP (10). Close underarm dart. Draw a short dart in the armhole. Note that this would not be attractive if gathered because there is a slight hollow at that point on the body and it is also a long way from the BP.

(e) Transfer underarm dart to shoulder and make it into short tucks (5). This is another instance where gathers do not work because the bust is not close enough. In fact as you will discover later, the gathers can be brought down onto the bust with the use of a yoke.

Finally, for interest, draw curved lines on 10 and 5, curving slightly along each side of the shaping, down to BP and out again along waist dart edges. Now you have learned another principle of designing: darts and shaping can not only be tucked or gathered, they can also be taken out in a seam. No matter what you do, the pattern will still fit.

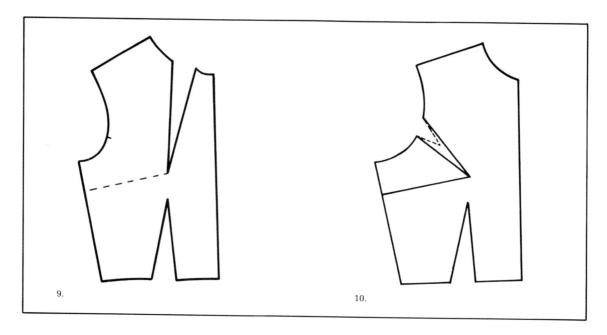

9.

10.

GRAIN

You will have noticed that if you put all the bust shaping in one place, that part of the pattern is distorted and if you keep CF on the SG another edge will be on the bias. This is perfectly acceptable provided your fabric is a plain or an all-over design, or if cutting it like this produces the particular effect you want. If it looks wrong either keep a small dart somewhere else in addition to the main one, or try cutting the bodice on the bias, either with a seam at CF or cutting it one piece.

EDGES

After transferring a dart to a new position, decide on length of dart, fold and pin and cut along pattern edge. When opened out the edge will be the correct shape. If the edge is to be tucked, proceed in the same way, folding the tucks into position. If the edge is to be gathered, draw a new smooth curved line slightly outside the original to allow some ease. Often one corner of pattern will extend further than

the others, these can be trimmed off by the new curve.

Have a look at ready-made clothes and see if you can see where the bust shaping is. This will also give you ideas for designing. In some stretch or jersey fabrics the bust dart may have been dispensed with altogether, you can do this yourself by folding it away to nothing across the pattern but make sure you then cut out with plenty of seam allowance just in case you have made it too tight or you overestimated the amount of stretch in the fabric.

Your decision about placing the bust shaping will depend upon the overall design. For instance if you are going to lower the neckline and cut away the armholes, you cannot put the bust dart in the shoulders. If you plan a front strap facing and low level pockets, it would be wise to move the waist dart away to reduce bulk and keep the bodice flat for the pockets, or gather it along the waist, or on a dress, cut it without a waist join and either belt in the shaping or wear it loose.

Designs Using the Bodice Block

This is undoubtedly the most interesting area for designing. There is scope for experimenting and, in addition, more style features are concentrated on the bodice than anywhere else.

Necklines

The neckline on the bodice block is shaped to fit around the base of the neck; you have read in an earlier section of the book how to alter it for individual postures. Unless a collar is added this is not a particularly flattering neckline and for most designs you will want to alter the front at least. You can draw the neckline to whatever shape you like and practice will show you which lines look good and which do not. Apart from being flattering, the neckline must be comfortable and lie flat and the garment should not fall off the shoulders. It helps to place back and front blocks together with shoulders meeting, back dart already in place but bust darts not yet moved. Even if you are altering back or front neck only you will get a better idea of what you are doing by having the blocks together.

Another tip is to outline the block against the fold of a double piece of paper so that, before cutting the new neck, you can open out the pattern to make sure the line is smooth and not too low, or as so often happens with a square neck, too wide. Remember to note bra strap positions, height of bust etc., and also that a low neck is invariably looser than a higher one.

(a) V-NECK

Measure from front neck hollow on yourself down to desired depth. Mark this depth on the copy of the block. With blocks together at shoulders, draw the new neckline, preferably

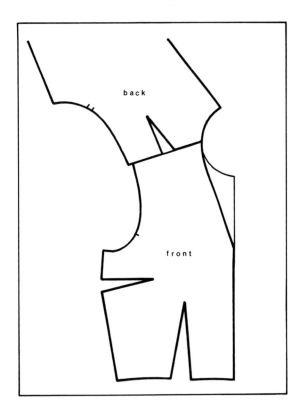

as a slight curve, following on from back neck. If you wish, the neck can be made slightly wider at the shoulder, sloping down to basic neckline at CB, or lowering it there as well. If you want a V at the back instead, follow the same procedure but you will have to lower the front neck as well by at least 1cm ($\frac{3}{8}$in), otherwise it will feel too high and tight and might pull up the back V.

Make the facing by measuring an even distance from the new neckline round back and front with the two still together. Mark balance marks. Trace off the facing; include the shoulder line. Mark the SG to match bodice, cut facing along shoulder. Mark CB and CF on facings. Add seam allowances to bodice and facings, mark FOLD where appropriate, CUT 1, CUT 2 etc.

(b) LOW NECK

Although a gaping neckline can be rectified after cutting out, by raising the shoulder or inserting darts or gathers, this changes the style. It is better to eliminate the gape beforehand as follows:

Outline blocks and place front against back with shoulders together. Draw the neckline shape required and check that it is correct. Do this by tracing it and trying it on or by measuring a garment with a similar neckline. Rule a line from BP to neckline. Cut out the neckline and cut the dart along the line to BP. Overlap or fold out a small dart in the neck, about 1cm ($\frac{3}{8}$in), allowing the bust dart to open further. This tightens the neckline and although the bust dart is slightly wider at the base it does not alter the fit because it is simply a little of the general ease across the chest that is being moved.

Reshape neck curve and trim the edge. A low back neck can be prevented from gaping by keeping it higher than the shoulder blade protrusion, by putting the dart in the neckline and folding it flat, tapering to nothing, before drawing the neckline.

Draw and trace facings as for (a) above, cut out facings and bodice adding seam allowances, mark SG, CB, CF and FOLD where appropriate.

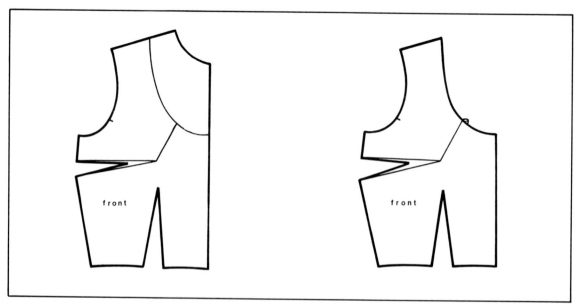

(c) LOW NECK SLEEVELESS BODICE

Outline front and back blocks. Draw neckline with blocks together at shoulders and also draw new armhole. This can be done by taking a small, even amount off all round front and back alike or by taking more off the shoulders for a cut-away line.

Outline facing by curving a line from above bust dart across to CF and CB. Trace off facings, mark CB and CF FOLD and mark the bodice appropriately. Cut all pieces adding seam allowances.

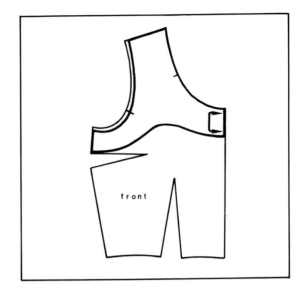

Edge Finishes

Depending on your design, neck and armhole edge can be finished in various ways. If the garment is to be lined you can mark the pattern to be cut in lining as well as fabric and attach the two by stitching round the neck and turning them RS out.

Another alternative is to bind the edges. There is no need to cut a pattern for bias strips unless you plan to use a lot of them in various places and you need to calculate the amount of fabric. Work out how much bias you need for a neck or armhole by measuring around the pattern edge, with tape measure on edge. The third method of finishing edges requires a pattern as follows.

FACINGS

These are often called shaped facings because one edge of the pattern follows that of the garment pattern. The outer edge of a facing is sometimes parallel with the garment edge, a convenient width is about 4–5cm ($1\frac{1}{2}$–2in).

Adapt the bodice to the style required, then put the patterns together at the shoulders. If the edge to be faced is straight and you are not intending to insert trimming in the seam or make the facing in a contrast colour, you may find you can simply add on an extension to make a fold-back facing. If not, cut an extra pattern piece, shaping the ends to match the garment when facing is folded back in position. Add seam allowances all round. Mark SG in same direction as garment or on the bias. A crossway strip of fabric used to bind or even face an edge, is really a narrow facing cut on the bias, trimmed to length after attaching.

To make a shaped facing which can be placed on the wrong side of the garment or the right side, and can only be seen on that side, use the pattern pieces to determine the shape. The illustration shows neck and armhole facings but the principle applies to all edges.

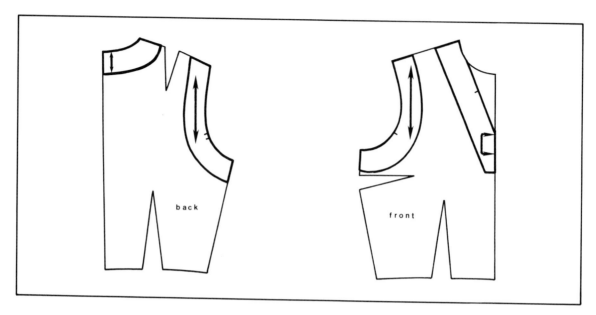

Mark the shape of the facing on the finished neck or armhole edge on the pattern. Draw a line parallel with the edge. A facing is usually 5–7cm (2–2$\frac{3}{4}$in) wide. Try to avoid darts. If there is a neck dart in the pattern, fold it out flat before marking the facing. Place the pattern on top of another piece of paper and outline the entire facing shape with your toothed tracing wheel, transferring it to the paper beneath. Pencil over the perforations, mark FOLD, SG, balance marks as appropriate. Cut out the facing, adding seam allowances.

Note that it may be advisable to fold the paper and therefore finish up with a complete facing pattern to be cut on a single fabric. It is a way of ensuring a good curve, a small piece of paper placed to a fold can result in a stepped edge. It is also advisable with an edge that is likely to stretch, such as a V neck, and here again, the final shape may be more accurate.

Reduce the number of seams where possible by placing small facing pieces together, such as back and front armhole. Mark SG to correspond with back of garment.

Facing patterns can also be used for cutting out interfacing. In fact when using iron-on Vilene/Pellon an excellent technique is to cut out the Vilene/Pellon pieces before the fabric, place the Vilene/Pellon adhesive side down on to WS of fabric, arranged as a single layer. Press the Vilene/Pellon to make it adhere then cut out round the outer edges using Vilene/Pellon edge as a guide. This saves getting adhesive on the iron as well as being less fiddly to do than lining up small pieces of fabric and interfacing.

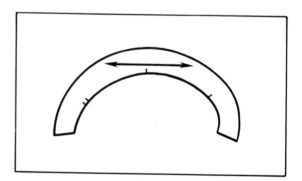

Armholes

Armholes can be changed in the same way as necklines although scope is more limited. The armhole on the basic pattern is the correct shape and size for a set-in sleeve and a certain amount of ease has been allowed to prevent the seam from splitting. If you are designing a sleeveless garment you would find the basic armhole a bit too low.

(a) SLEEVELESS FITTED BODICE

Outline back and front block. Raise underarm point on each by 1.5cm ($\frac{5}{8}$in) and re-draw the armhold curve to this point. Mark another point 1.5cm ($\frac{5}{8}$in) inside edge of seam, fold out the dart and re-draw the side seam from the new underarm point. Place back and front together to check seam.

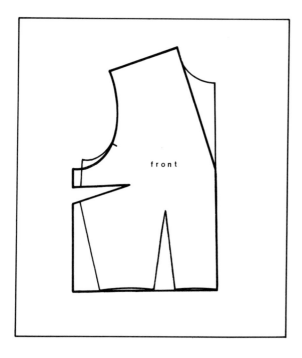

(b) SLEEVELESS LOOSE-FIT BODICE

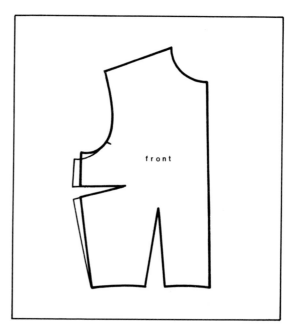

When using the block for a looser top or for a garment to be worn over another the armhole should be looser and the garment bigger.

Lower the armhole on back and front by 1.5cm ($\frac{5}{8}$in) or whatever is needed to lower it beneath the seam of the blouse etc., to be worn underneath. Add an extra 1.5cm ($\frac{5}{8}$in) at the underarm point to make bodice wider and re-draw armhole and side seam line at the waist, loosening the bodice all the way to the waist. Put back and front together to check side seam edges.

You may also wish to cut away the armhole slightly at the shoulders. To do this, place back and front together with shoulders meeting and redraw. Remember that any reduction makes a looser fit and it may gape if you take off too much.

(c) CAP SLEEVE

This is a useful adaptation to learn. It is comfortable to wear as it covers the top of the arm and is therefore flattering.

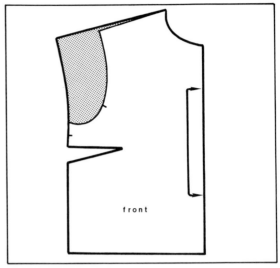

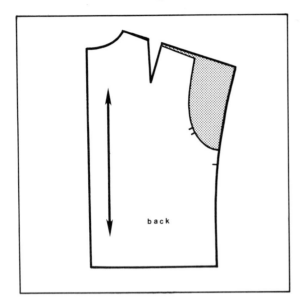

Outline back and front bodice block. Mark a point 1cm ($\frac{3}{8}$in) above the shoulder seam at armhole edge. Rule new shoulder seams through these points. Mark a balance mark 3cm ($1\frac{1}{4}$in) below armhole. Put back and front together with shoulders meeting and draw a new armhole edge for the cap sleeve, curving it in on the front and out on the back for a good line.

When making it up stitch the side seams as far as the balance mark. The armholes can be faced or they can be finished with a narrow hem. If you prefer a wide hem draw a straight armhole edge on the cap sleeve and add an extra extension 4cm ($1\frac{1}{2}$in) wide from shoulder to 2cm ($\frac{3}{4}$in) below balance mark.

Cut-off Tops

These are very useful adaptations to learn as they can be used for underwear and nightwear as well as strappy evening and sun-dresses and camisole tops to wear under jackets.

(a) CAMISOLE TOP

Outline back and front bodice block, including underarm dart. For a low style draw a line across back at underarm level or a little below, continue on to front for a short distance before curving it up to a rise over the bust. This will in fact be a straight edge after the dart has been put in. Extend side seams to lengthen pattern if required longer than waist length, allowing for casing if needed. Draw straight hem lines.

Put back and front together at shoulders and draw the strap, making one edge run from edge of dart on back shoulder. Trace off straps;

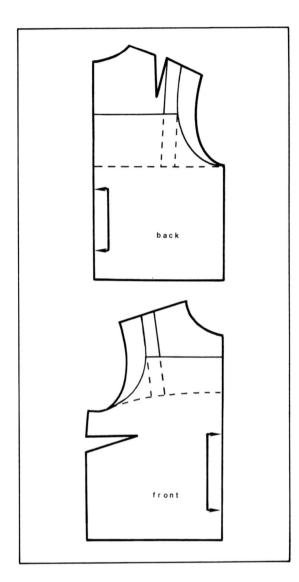

Notes

1. Except in underwear and nightwear the upper edge will need interfacing. Use the facing pattern and cut soft iron-on or sew-in Vilene/Pellon 1cm ($\frac{3}{8}$in) narrower than the pattern.

2. The lower style works well if lined instead of being faced. In some fabrics it could be lined with self fabric.

3. Make straps 3cm ($1\frac{1}{4}$ in) wide finished so that they can be interfaced with lightweight Fold-a-Band/Fuse'n'Fold/Waist-Shaper.

(b) PETTICOAT TOP

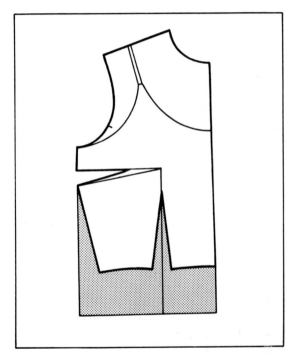

mark and trace facings for upper edge of camisole. Add seam allowances and CF, CB and FOLD where appropriate.

For a higher upper edge rule a line on front and back at the level you want it. Scoop out the armholes, establishing the width of the top edge of the front and back by measuring on the body to just beyond bra strap. Put patterns together with shoulders matching and draw the strap between the two corners. Draw and trace off facings, mark back and front with CF, CB and FOLD as appropriate.

For a top with bust darts, outline the bodice back and front, with underarm and waist dart. Lengthen if required. Draw strap position, measuring on the body to coincide with bra strap. Draw a curved neckline and scoop out the armhole. The upper edge could be faced but binding is another alternative. Re-cut, adding seam allowances and mark CB, CF and FOLD.

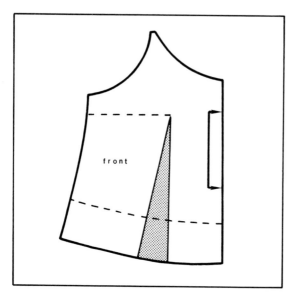

Notes

1. The back may be shaped to match the front or it could be straight across at underarm. For a loose style that could be a night-dress or sun-dress or a garment with a draw-string waist, outline the front block, draw neckline and armhole then close the underarm dart. This transfers all the shaping into the waist and swings the side seam out. Extend the CF and side seams to length required. On the back pattern draw the neck-line and armhole then shape the side seam to a similar angle from the underarm. This can be done by putting the back on top of the front. It is also a good opportunity to check the length of the side edges. Draw smooth hem-line curves. Cut out pattern, adding seam allowances, mark CB, CF and FOLD.

2. If you draw a low front neckline, take a small pleat from the neckline as described under (b) low neck on page 66. This will have the advantage of increasing the flare in the lower edge even more.

3. This style can be cut on the bias. To do this, fold a piece of paper before cutting the pattern, then open it out to reveal the whole front or back and draw SG at 45 degrees to the centre fold.

4. If you require more flare, cut the pattern from hem to mid-neck and open out the pieces to insert extra width at the hemline. Place on new paper and outline.

Yokes

Yokes are style features that provide the opportunity to introduce emphasis in the form of top stitching, contrast colour etc. The yoke also provides an extra seam that can be used as a fitting point and a place for adding features such as gathers and tucks or more fullness for a particular reason.

(a) SHALLOW YOKE

On basic bodice eg., shirt-style.
    Outline back and front bodice blocks. Draw front yoke line from neckline to armhole. This can be parallel with shoulder seam or sloping down towards armhole. The back yoke is usually deeper than the front to provide the correct balance and to bring the shaping down onto the shoulder blades. Mark two balance marks across each yoke line. Cut off the yokes.

Back: Close the shoulder dart and the lower edge will rise. This has transferred the dart into the yoke seam but if you leave it like this the shape will not look right: ideally both edges should be slightly shaped so cut a small

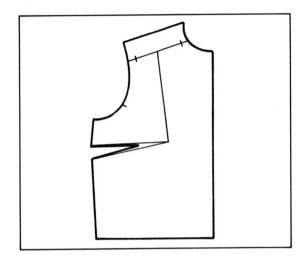

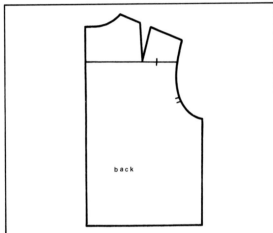

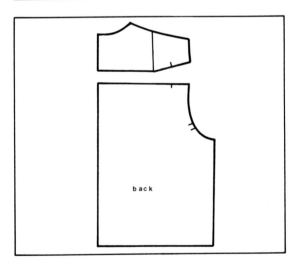

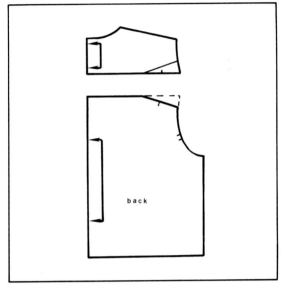

wedge shape from the lower edge and join it to the yoke. Re-cut both pieces adding seam allowances. Mark CF, CB and FOLD. Mark CUT 1 and on the yoke, CUT 1 in interfacing if required.

Front: Close underarm dart and allow it to open at the yoke edge. Ignore the waist dart. Re-draw upper edge of bodice as a smooth curve. Place on fresh paper and outline, adding seam allowances. Mark SG on bodice and yoke.

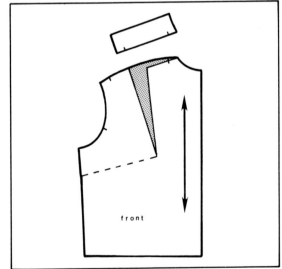

Note

You may want to add a collar, front fastening etc., so refer to appropriate sections for this and for lengthening to hip length etc.

(b) SHALLOW YOKE AND GATHERS eg., BLOUSE

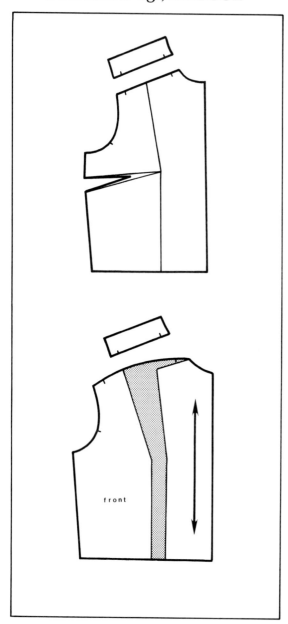

Follow instructions under (a) above but having transferred the front dart into the upper edge of the bodice, cut to lower edge, spread the pieces and insert additional width for gathers. Keep the edges parallel below the BP and insert $\frac{1}{4}$ of the total you need. This could be from 2–7cm ($\frac{3}{4}$–$2\frac{3}{4}$in) depending on the type of fabric to be used. Outline the new pattern adding seam allowances and mark the pattern appropriately.

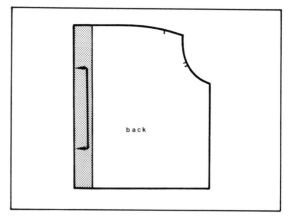

If the yoke is straight, fullness can be added to the back bodice by extending at the CB edge, otherwise cut the pattern in two places and spread the pieces to insert the extra required.

(c) ONE-PIECE YOKE eg., SADDLE YOKE

To avoid having three seams close together, eliminate the shoulder seam by placing back and front yoke together with shoulder seams together, outline again round both pieces. Cut out adding seam allowances. Mark CB FOLD.

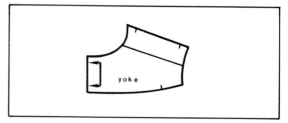

The front yoke edges will not be on the straight grain, which can look attractive.

(d) SHALLOW FRONT YOKE ONLY

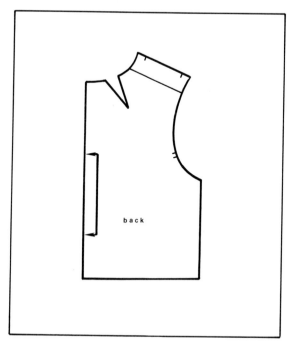

This style uses the block back as it is, fullness is added to the front only. Adapt front block as described under (a) above, cut off the yoke. On the back block transfer the shoulder dart to the neck. Place front yoke against back block with shoulder edges together. Outline the whole, adding seam allowances.

(e) SHAPED YOKE

The illustration shows a curved yoke but it can be square. A shaped yoke is deep, bringing the fullness down nearer to the bust. Outline back and front bodice block, lengthen if required. Draw yoke line from underarm round to CB and CF edges. Add balance mark, trace off yoke and mark FOLD, CUT 1 or CUT 2 if lined, and CUT 1 in interfacing.

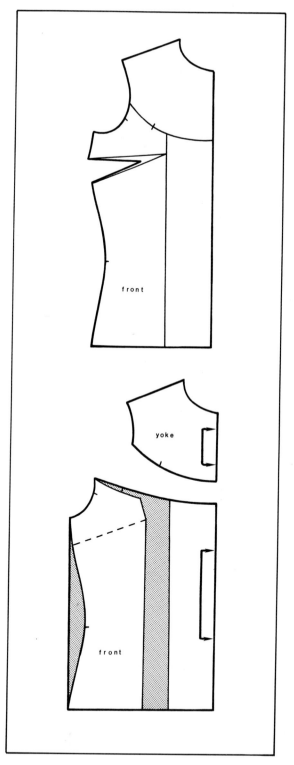

Back: Cut through dart from shoulder to lower edge of yoke, close dart. Re-draw yoke with new curved edge.

Front: Rule vertical line from yoke edge to hem, passing through BP. Close underarm dart to transfer it to yoke edge. Cut remainder of vertical line and spread out the pieces inserting $\frac{1}{4}$ of the total required for the garment. On the new pattern, add seam allowances and mark CF, FOLD.

(f) DEEP YOKE AND FLARED SKIRT

The illustration shows a flared lower section which entails ensuring that the upper edge fits the yoke. The neckline has been lowered and the armhole scooped out but this can be varied. This adaptation is especially useful for maternity clothes and also nightwear.

Outline the block and adapt neck and armhole. Draw yoke seam along upper edge of dart and on to the CF. Insert balance marks. Put back against front with side seams together and draw the back yoke seam at the same level as the front. Cut patterns along yoke lines. Re-draw yokes adding seam allowances. Mark CF FOLD and CUT 1 or if to be lined, mark appropriately. Note that you may have to put a seam at CB for a zipper. If neck and armholes are to be faced, outline the edges and trace off the facing including neck and armhole area as one facing.

On lower part of pattern lengthen as required and rule a straight side seam. Divide into three with vertical lines, cut on the lines and spread out inserting extra width at the hem in the first two spaces. At side seam add half the amount. Re-curve the hemline. Add flare to back and front alike.

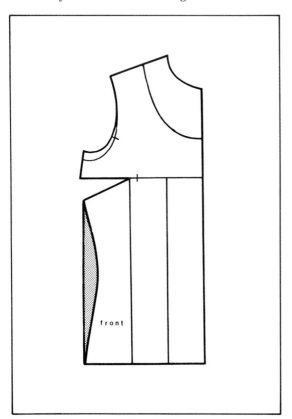

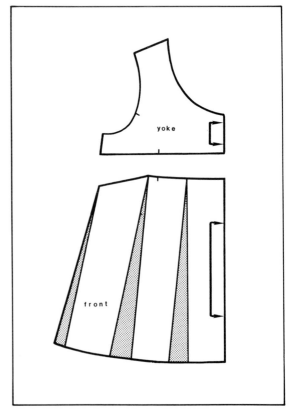

Seams as Style Lines

The shaping put into the block by means of darts can be concealed in seams that run through the darts and the length of the pattern. These styles are easier to fit as the adjustment can be more detailed. Sometimes the seam is used decoratively, away from dart positions, in which case the dart may still be required. An example of this would occur if the back darts are in the neck of the block to provide a good shape for the figure but the vertical seam would run from mid-shoulder to hem, taking in the waist dart but missing the neck dart. Remember to allow for a long opening in one of the seams.

(a) PRINCESS SEAMS

This term refers to vertical seams that run from mid-shoulder to hem. The illustration shows a style with a pleated hemline section. Use the bodice block extended to hip level.

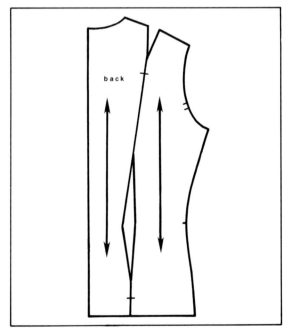

Back: Outline block; draw a line from point of shoulder dart to top of waist dart, through the dart and down to the hem. Insert balance marks across the line. Cut along sides of darts and along seam line but curving the edges gently rather than following the angles, and providing less shaping rather than more. Trace off each piece separately, cut out adding seam allowances. Mark SG down the middle of each and label CB panel and SIDE panel respectively. (CB may be cut with a seam for a zipper to be inserted.) Make sure balance marks are transferred.

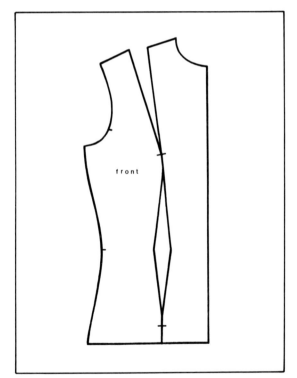

Front: Outline front block. Transfer underarm dart to shoulder. Draw a line to run along each side of the shoulder dart, down through BP and the middle of the waist dart and on to the hem. Insert balance marks across the line.

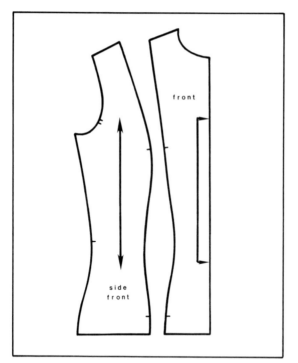

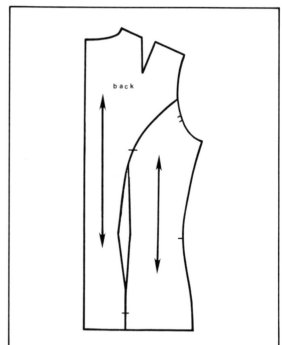

Cut along the line each side of each dart, curving gently. Trace each piece, label CF panel and SIDE front panel respectively. Mark CF FOLD. Draw SG down the middle of the side panel and make sure balance marks are transferred. Add seam allowances and cut out the pattern.

(b) CURVED PANEL SEAMS

With this style the vertical seams start in the armhole. You cannot get a really close fitting garment from this adaptation. Use the bodice block lengthened to hip or dress length.

Back: Draw a curved line from just above armhole balance mark down to hem passing through the middle of the waist dart. Insert balance marks above and below dart. Cut along the line each side of the dart in a curve. Trace off each section and label. Mark SG lines parallel with CB. (CB may be cut with a seam for a zipper.) The neck or shoulder dart is retained.

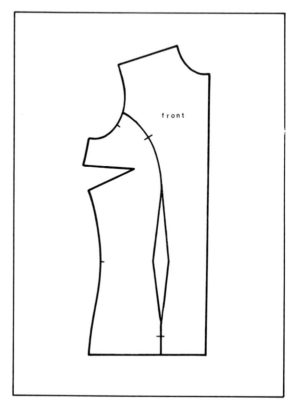

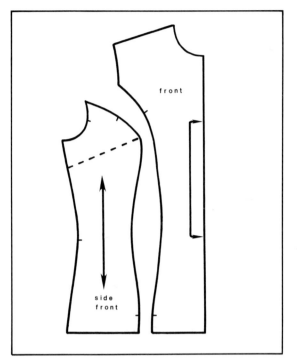

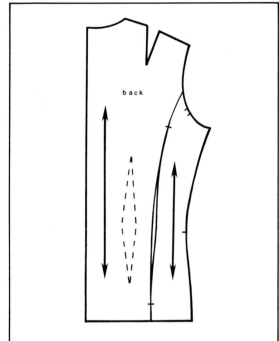

Front: Draw a curved line from just above armhole balance mark, bringing it over the BP, through it and down the middle of the dart to the hem. Insert balance marks across the line. Close the underarm dart to transfer it into the armhole. Cut along remainder of panel line curving it along each side of the waist dart. Trace off each section curving the side panel edge over the BP. Add seam allowances and SG; label it Side Front panel. Label CF panel and FOLD and cut out adding seam allowances.

(c) WIDE PANEL WITH BUST DART

The advantage of this seaming is that it retains a closer bust fit with a looser skirt, and also you are not restricted to a definite panel width. Use bodice block lengthened to hip or dress length.

Back: Draw a curved line from armhole and straight down to hem. Ignore the waist dart

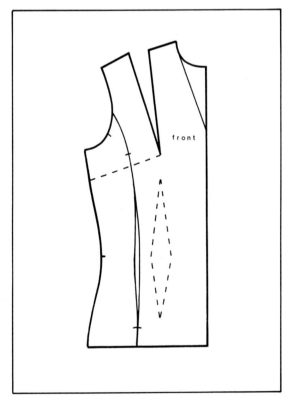

but put some shaping in the panel seam by curving it each side for some distance. Insert balance marks. Trace each piece, retaining the neck or shoulder dart. Transfer balance marks, mark SG and add seam allowances.

Front: Draw curved line from armhole, cutting through end of bust dart and on down to the hem. Insert balance marks. Transfer the waist dart to the seam line. Do this either by measuring or by tracing the dart and superimposing its size on the panel line. If you prefer a looser fit take a smaller amount out of the panel line. Trace off side panel, close the bust dart to transfer it into the armhole edge. Cut side panel adding seam allowances. Draw SG and label pattern. Trace CF panel including remains of bust dart. Label pattern and cut out adding seam allowances. The illustration shows a V-neck but it can be any neckline.

Note

The adaptations have been shown on a hip length block but they can all be done with a dress length block. Remember that pleats could be inserted with the panel lines if required.

(e) HIGH WAIST STYLE

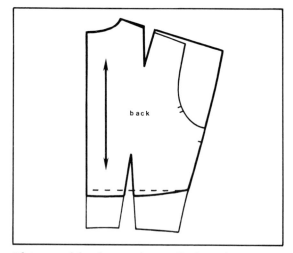

This could almost be called a low yoke because when making a yoke pattern, you use as much of the bodice shape as necessary for the upper part of the garment, and adapt what is left.

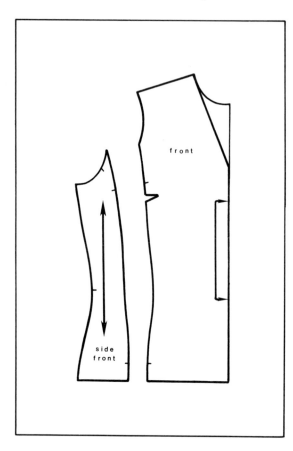

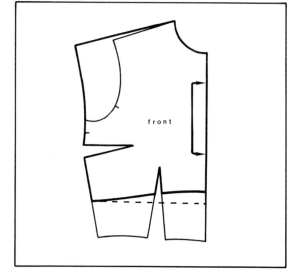

Outline front and back bodice block. Adapt neckline and armhole if necessary. Place patterns together at side seam and rule a guide line at right angles to CF and CB across both pieces at the same distance above waist edges. Draw a curved yoke seam taking it 2cm ($\frac{3}{4}$in) below guide line at CB and 2cm ($\frac{3}{4}$in) above it at CF. Insert balance marks. Cut along yoke line to separate bodice. Label bodice patterns and re-cut adding seam allowances.

To make skirt pattern place each lower bodice section on fresh paper and outline. Extend CF and CB lines to length required. Rule a vertical line from side edge above

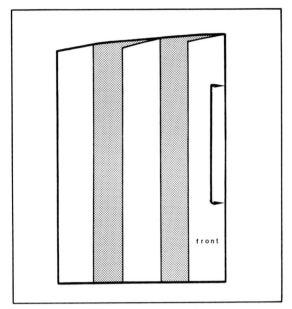

waist. Complete the rectangle. Rule two vertical lines to divide rectangle into three. Cut up each line, separate the pieces and outline on fresh paper inserting $\frac{1}{8}$ of the extra width you need for gathers. Redraw the waistline curve. Mark CF and CB FOLD. Alternatively make a CB seam on skirt and bodice for inserting a zipper. Add seam and hem allowances and cut out.

Note
If you prefer a flared skirt, cut on the guide lines and open out the sections at hem only, keeping the waist edge the same size as the bodice.

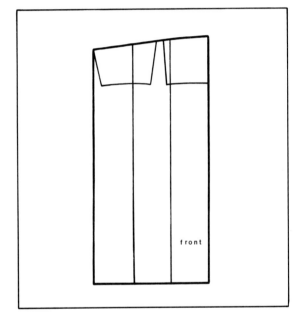

Adapting for Fastenings

There are many different types of overlapping openings but if you work through those that follow, you will understand the principles sufficiently to attempt other styles.

Remember the following general points:

1. The buttons or other fastening will be located on the CF line for a central opening, but as the bodice block ends on the CF line you must always add extra to the right half so that there will be some fabric beyond the button. The amount you add will depend on the design and on the size of the button. If you also add the same amount to the left or underside this will provide an overlapping opening.

2. Buttonholes can be horizontal but make sure the underlap is wide enough so that you cannot see through the buttonholes. Use vertical buttons only with a small underlap on loose garments.

3. The opening edges must be interfaced and faced. The facing can be a separate piece of fabric re-joined along the buttoned edge, or if the fabric is wide enough, the facing can be cut all in one and folded back before making the buttonholes. Insert the interfacing between the layers. Use the correct weight of iron-on or sew-in Vilene/Pellon attached to the garment unless it is likely to show. Try using lightest weight Vilene/Pellon and adding a strip of light Fold-a-Band/Fuse'n' Fold/Waist-Shaper pressed with the perforations along the fold line so that you have a good crisp fold when the facing is turned back. With a narrow overlap and small buttons the buttonholes fall on the Fold-a-Band/ Fuse'n'Fold/Waist-Shaper which provides extra support for them.

4. It is important to mark the CF line and the fold line on the pattern and on the fabric. When overlapped the CF lines must always be on top of each other.

5. The amount you add to the pattern beyond CF is normally referred to as the button stand or extension.

The following examples are illustrated on the bodice block with one dart only, at underarm. The instructions are the same whether for a dress, blouse, tunic etc., except that you should adapt the block to length and also adapt the neckline if necessary, before working out the opening. All instructions also apply to back fastenings.

(a) SIMPLE OPENING

Fold a piece of paper, place the front block on it with CF edge 1.5–2cm ($\frac{5}{8}$–$\frac{3}{4}$in) from the fold, or more for large buttons, a wider wrap-over or for heavy fabric. Outline the block. Mark buttonholes or fastening positions with top

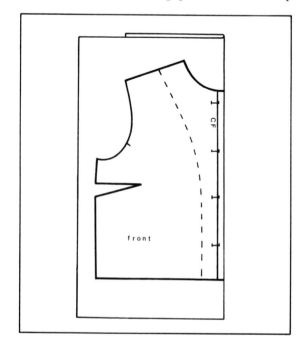

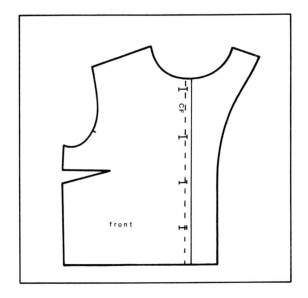

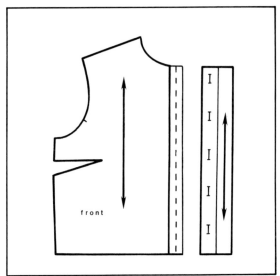

one at least 2cm ($\frac{3}{4}$in) below neck edge and bottom one above waistline. On a close fitting dress bodice locate a fastening level with BP. At shoulder and at hem measure 6–8cm ($2\frac{1}{2}$–$3\frac{1}{4}$in) from fold. Draw the curved line between the two as the facing edge. Run spiked tracing wheel along the line to penetrate paper beneath. Cut out the pattern, cut along perforated line. Mark CF, and FOLD LINE, label the pattern, draw SG parallel with CF. Cut out adding seam allowances.

Note

These instructions provide for a simple fold-back facing. If you wish to cut it separately, cut along fold after cutting out the pattern. Re-cut the pieces adding seam allowances all round.

(b) BAND OPENING

This is a classic shirt opening which is economical in fabric and allows for the use of contrast fabric for the band (and collar and cuffs of course). It is ideal for interfacing with Fold-a-Band/Fuse'n'Fold/Waist-Shaper only.

Outline bodice block, add 1.5cm ($\frac{5}{8}$in) to CF edge and draw another line 1.5cm ($\frac{5}{8}$in) inside

CF edge. Insert balance marks. This gives a band width of 3cm ($1\frac{1}{4}$in) which is right for Fold-a-Band/Fuse'n'Fold/Waist-Shaper. Cut off the 3cm ($1\frac{1}{4}$in) strip and draw it again double that width, placing to fold of paper for ease. Mark buttonholes vertically in the middle of one half. Mark the centre of strip FOLD LINE and label pattern BAND. Draw SG parallel with centre line. With paper folded place on bodice block and trace curve of neckline. Cut across top of band, adding seam allowance to produce correct shape. Add seam allowance all round and also to edge of bodice pattern.

Notes

1. Band can be cut on bias grain for contrast effect in checks etc.

2. If shirt fabric is the same on both sides eg., poplin, the band can be cut in one with the shirt front and simply folded onto the RS to be stitched down. The band on the left shirt front would be turned to WS as a hem.

3. It is usual to attach a separate band to the right shirt front only, the left side is concealed and a band might make unnecessary bulk. Cut a separate left front pattern with 3cm ($1\frac{1}{4}$in) added to CF edge for a hem. Remember to mark each pattern CUT 1.

(c) STRAP OPENING

The instructions are for a rectangular strap on a garment cut to a CF fold but the strap can be pointed at the bottom and the garment can have a seam, which makes it easier to construct. This is a useful opening if you haven't enough fabric for a full length, wide facing. Make the strap 6cm ($2\frac{1}{2}$in) wide ie., 3cm ($1\frac{1}{4}$in) finished, so that you can interface it with Fold-a-Band/Fuse'n'Fold/Waist-Shaper.

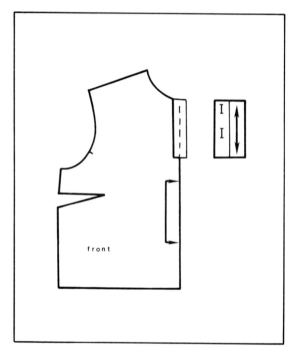

Outline the bodice block. Measure length of opening down from neck. Add 1.5cm ($\frac{5}{8}$in) to CF edge for button stand and draw a line 1.5cm ($\frac{5}{8}$in) inside CF line. Insert balance mark. Cut out the rectangle. Label remainder of pattern and mark CF FOLD. Add seam allowances. Cut strap double width, mark centre FOLD, SG and buttonholes. Copy neck curve from block and cut out adding seam allowances and label it CUT 2.

Note
Strap can be cut on the bias for distinctive effect.

(d) DOUBLE BREASTED STYLE

The illustration shows the block adapted to a yoke.

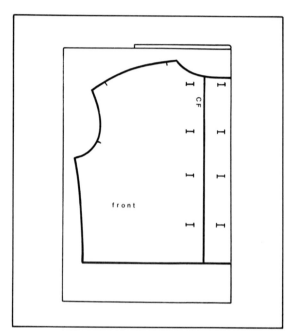

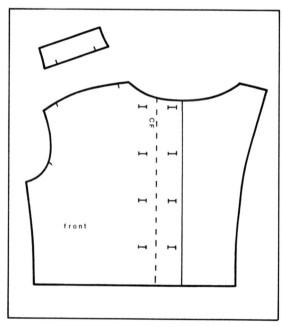

Outline the block and mark 2 rows of buttons, one each side of CF, spaced to look well-balanced. Draw a line 1.5–2cm ($\frac{5}{8}$–$\frac{3}{4}$in) beyond the outer row of buttons or buttonholes. To cut with a fold-back facing place this front on a folded piece of paper and outline it, transferring all marks. Use a spiked tracing wheel to mark the facing edge extending from well inside inner row of buttonholes to yoke line or shoulder. Cut out pattern, cut along perforated line. Mark CF and FOLD LINE. Mark SG parallel with CF.

If you prefer a separate facing, add a seam allowance to the edge nearest outer row of buttons. Trace facing to correct width as before.

Note

If this pattern is used for a jacket, with a pointed collar and convertible lapel fastening, the outer edge beyond the buttons looks better curved slightly outwards. A separate facing with similar edge would be required.

(e) ASSYMETRICAL FASTENING

Many interesting designs can be made applying the same principles of extending the edge and making sure it is double, but cutting the right and left sides of the pattern separately. Remember to label each CUT 1. These patterns are not usually very economical but the left, or underside need not have a wide facing as it remains concealed. It is simplest if you keep the fastening edge away from the darts.

Fold a piece of paper and outline the bodice block with CF on the fold. Outline the block with spiked tracing wheel, cut out and open out the pattern. Mark CF line as a guide. Draw the fastening edge in a suitable position. Insert balance marks; mark the buttonholes etc., where you want them. Rule a line 2cm ($\frac{3}{4}$in) or more beyond that and cut out the pattern on that line. Place right front pattern with the edge on the fold of a piece of paper and out-

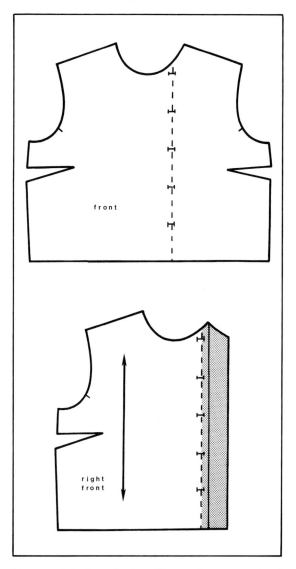

line it. Mark a facing line using a toothed tracing wheel. The illustration shows a straight facing. If the corner is to be folded back as rever, draw a sloped facing up to the shoulder edge. The shaded area indicates the extent of interfacing needed. Cut out the pattern, cut on perforated line, mark FOLD LINE and buttonholes. Draw SG parallel with CF; add seam allowances. Label pattern CUT 1.

Take left front and place on folded paper. Add button stand and allowance to edge and draw facing to match right front. Use the right

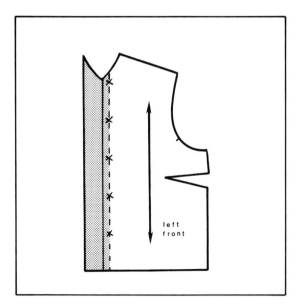

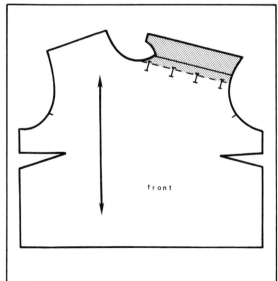

front pattern placed on top of left as a guide to getting the measurements the same. Cut out, adding seam allowances. Mark FOLD LINE, button positions and SG.

(f) HORIZONTAL OPENING

Cut out entire front as described for (e) above. Draw opening edge. Insert balance marks and button positions as before, add button stand

and cut out right front. Add facing extension 5–6cm (2–2$\frac{1}{2}$in) wide using folded paper in order to get a shaped edge at neck and armhole. Keep the pattern folded and place left front pattern on folded paper with the edge far enough from fold to make it match the right front. Mark facing width, cut out and open out pattern. Add seam allowances to both pieces. Mark SG parallel with CF on both pieces. Shading on illustration indicates area to be interfaced. Mark each pattern CUT 1.

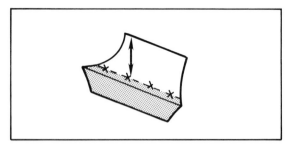

Notes

1. The style illustrated is an excellent one for fastening with Velcro Spot-Ons.

2. If the neckline is also to be faced mark a shaped facing, while pattern pieces are on folded paper, extending right round neck to shoulder edge.

SLEEVE DESIGNS

The sleeve with the basic block is long and fitted with an elbow dart. Use it to alter it to fit and to establish the correct length. There are few occasions when you will need a sleeve like that so it is useful to convert it to a straight pattern without darts and make a cardboard block that is ready to use for full sleeves. Sleeve adaptations are easy: remember to retain the special shape of the sleeve head even when it includes gathers.

(a) STRAIGHT SLEEVE BLOCK

Outline the fitted block and cut it out. Cut along centre line from waist to elbow line. Cut along dart to centre line. Fold out the dart to allow it to open at the wrist. Redraw the sleeve, ruling new side seams straight from underarm. Redraw curve at wrist. Check seam edges are equal in length. Transfer balance marks, SG and elbow line.

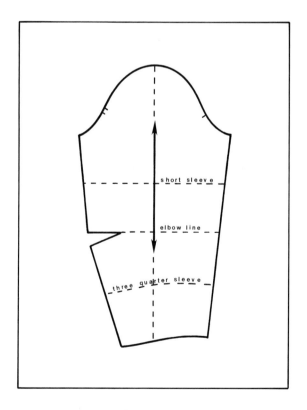

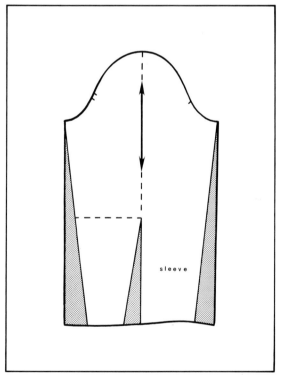

(b) PLAIN SHORT SLEEVES

The simplest of all sleeve adaptations ie., shortening, is done by cutting the block shorter. It is useful to have a line for a short and a three-quarter sleeve marked on both blocks. Measure the seams of existing garments as a guide to the position of these lines. The three-quarter length line must be curved parallel with wrist edge. Measure each seam edge to make sure hemline is accurate.

(c) SHIRT SLEEVE

This is a long sleeve with smooth head and a small amount of fullness gathered or pleated into a cuff. Decide on depth of cuff. If you

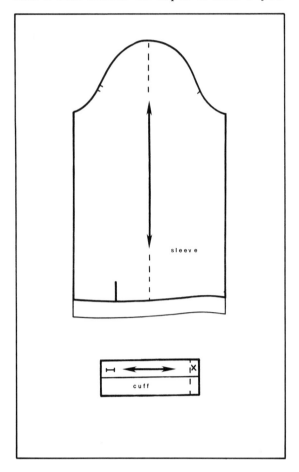

intend to use Fold-a-Band/Fuse'n'Fold/Waist-Shaper the cuff should be 3cm ($1\frac{1}{4}$in) deep.

Outline straight sleeve block. Shorten it by desired cuff depth. Draw a line for position of opening mid-way between centre line and back of sleeve ie., edge at left. The opening should be 7–9cm ($2\frac{3}{4}$–$3\frac{1}{2}$in) long. Re-draw the sleeve adding seam allowances. Transfer balance marks and SG line. To make cuff pattern, draw a rectangle twice the depth of piece taken from block and in length make it wrist measurement plus 5cm (2in) ease. Add to this 1.5–2cm ($\frac{5}{8}$–$\frac{3}{4}$in) for underlap for fastening. Alternatively cut a piece of Fold-a-Band/ Fuse'n'Fold/Waist-Shaper to length. It is worth keeping a note of your cuff length to save having to measure it each time. Re-draw pattern adding seam allowances. Mark SG along its length, mark centre fold line, extension and button and buttonhole position. Mark wrist edge with dotted line for gathers or draw three or four small tucks. Calculate amount to be tucked by subtracting cuff length from sleeve wrist edge length.

(d) SHORT PUFF SLEEVE

This sleeve is gathered into the armhole and gathered at the lower edge into a band.

Outline straight sleeve block to short sleeve length. Rule lines to divide it into four equal sections. For a very full sleeve in fine fabric divide it into six. Cut along each line to separate the sections. Spread them out and insert

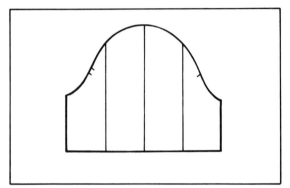

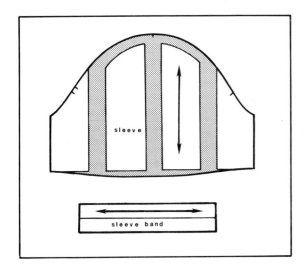

(e) FLARED SLEEVE

This style has a smooth sleeve head but is full at the hemline.

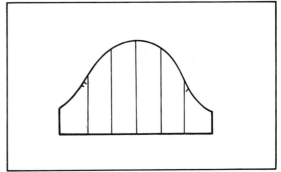

the same amount of additional fullness in each gap. The amount can be 3–5cm (1¼–2in) but keep an eye on the total width especially if using 90cm (36in) wide fabric. To add extra length to allow the gathering to stand up, add 1–2cm (⅜–¾in) at centre of sleeve head and draw a new sleeve head curve from there to the original underarm points. Redraw lower edge curving it below the sections. Redraw the pattern marking SG down centre. Mark gathering line between balance marks at sleeve head. Mark gathers along lower edge to stop short of the edges. Add seam allowances.

Cut sleeve band pattern to fit upper arm plus 5cm (2in) ease plus twice finished depth. Add seam allowances.

Notes

1. This sleeve can have elastic at the hem instead of a cuff. Add sufficient hem allowance to form casing.

2. An elbow length or below elbow sleeve can be made in the same way, cutting the band pattern to appropriate length.

3. Make sleeve bands 6cm (2½ in) wide if you intend using Fold-a-Band/Fuse'n'Fold/Waist-Shaper.

Outline straight sleeve block to short or elbow length. Rule vertical lines to divide sleeve into 6 sections. Cut up the lines almost to the sleeve head edge and spread out the pieces, opening them at lower edge only. Insert as much as you think you can for the fabric being used. This sleeve will not fit on folded 90cm (36in) fabric.

Outline sleeve on fresh paper. Transfer balance marks. Draw SG down centre or the sleeve can be cut on the bias, in which case mark SG at 45 degrees. Cut out allowing seam allowances and a hem at lower edge.

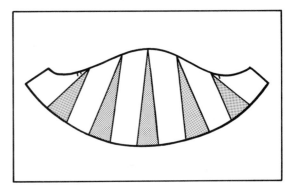

Notes

1. This style of sleeve can also be gathered into a band. Cut the band as described above for (d).

2. This is attractive if made in 2 layers of contrasting fabric.

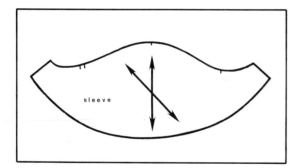

(f) LONG FULL SLEEVE, ELASTIC WRIST AND FRILL OR RUFFLE

This sleeve is full at the wrist and requires extra length for the frilled or ruffled hem.

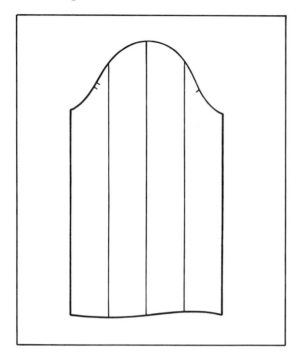

Outline straight sleeve block and rule vertical lines to divide sleeve into four. Cut up the lines almost to the sleeve head edge. Open out the pieces spreading them to open at wrist only. Place on fresh paper and outline. Calculate depth of frill or ruffle and also add 1cm ($\frac{3}{8}$ in) for elastic casing. Add seam allowances;

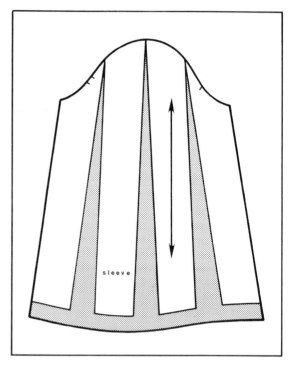

mark SG down centre of sleeve; transfer balance marks.

Note
This sleeve can be made fuller by dividing it into 6 and spreading the sections at the back further to add more fullness. If you also make the sleeve longer by 4–5cm (2in), excluding frill or ruffle, it will hang from the arm in a very attractive shape. Make sure seam edges are equal in length.

(g) SLEEVE WITH GATHERED HEAD

This adaptation can be made to a short or long fitted sleeve.

Outline fitted sleeve block to required length. Rule a line across sleeve just above sleeve head balance marks. Divide upper section into 5 segments. Cut out the sleeve, cut along segment lines to centre. Open out the pieces inserting extra fullness between edges.

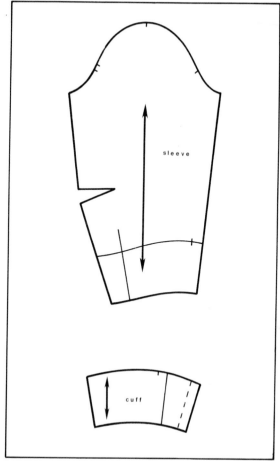

Outline on fresh paper. Re-draw sleeve head in a smooth curve, transfer balance marks. Add SG. Mark gathering position between balance marks or draw four tucks to correspond with the added amounts.

Note

To keep high gathered heads in position re-inforce by making up with crisp lining backing the sleeve, or press a piece of soft iron-on Vilene/Pellon to WS of sleeve head after cutting out fabric.

(h) FULL SLEEVE WITH SHAPED CUFF

With this style fullness is added at head and wrist.

Outline fitted sleeve block. Decide on depth of cuff and draw a curved line across sleeve, measuring up evenly from wrist. Mark position of opening mid-way between centre and back edge, extending it above cuff line by 4cm (1½in). Insert a balance mark across the cuff line. Cut off the cuff section. Cut along opening line of cuff and re-assemble the two pieces with the sleeve seam edges together. Outline the cuff, transferring the balance mark. Add 1.5cm (⅝in) extension for fastening to back edge of cuff. Add seam allowances all round and cut out. Mark SG down centre. Try this cuff around wrist, you may need to shorten it if a close fit is required. To do this, cut on the seam line and overlap. Mark the pattern CUT 4 as it has a seam along outer edge.

On main part of sleeve, cut along dart to opening line and down to wrist. Close dart. Cut sleeve into four and spread out on fresh paper, inserting extra at sleeve head and wrist

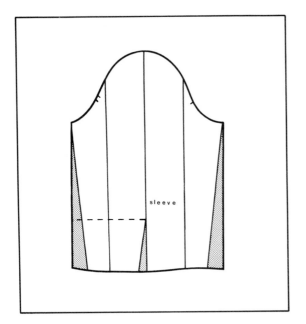
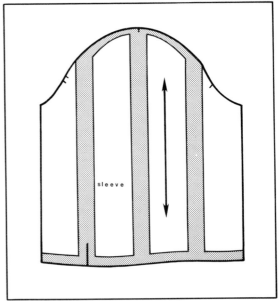

as for (d) Puff Sleeve. Redraw sleeve head and wrist in smooth curves. Transfer balance marks, mark SG down centre of sleeve. Mark opening at lower edge 4cm ($1\frac{1}{2}$in) long or mark two small clips 1cm ($\frac{3}{8}$in) long and 2cm ($\frac{3}{4}$in) apart for a simple fold-back opening.

GENERAL FEATURES

There are a number of items that can be used as functional or decorative features on a variety of garments. The patterns for these features are cut according to standard rules and instructions, often even the measurements are the same no matter what the garment. For example, although a waistband can vary in width and can even be shaped, the length must be standard ie., when overlapped and fastened it must be waist size; a pocket used to put things in must be big enough for the hand to go in; a collar can be any shape or size but the length of the neckline edge must always equal the length of the garment neckline, and so on.

Collars

Collars are most enjoyable to draft yourself for many reasons. The pattern piece is small so it is easy to see the shape you are creating; it can be quickly tried around your neck or on the dummy and it takes only a few minutes to cut another one if necessary; it is probably the only place where you can give free rein to your imagination and be as frivolous or outrageous as you like; the collar is a good point of focus to draw attention away from figure problems elsewhere, and finally, while the fabric is very important and often restricting in other parts of a garment, for a collar you can use all sorts of fabrics — transparent, filmy, stiff, floppy, springy, fraying, white, plain, patterned, cheap, expensive, discreet or bizarre without hesitation.

The principles involved in making collar patterns are the same for all styles so once you have made a few and understand them, there will be no limit to what you can do. Collar shapes change with fashion so it is not possible to show how to draft all types but those that are described below represent the main ones. For instance, a basic pointed collar for a blouse or shirt is shown but from time to time fashion decrees that the points should be short, long, upturned etc., but you will still be able to use the instructions in this book because the principle remains unchanged.

Most collars are cut in one piece, the ends coming together at CF, CB or to one side at the front; a few are in two pieces such as the Peter Pan collar; some are cut in one piece and joined before attaching to the neckline such as a polo collar. Other collars include those that have extended ends to tie, those that are frilled, ruffled or fluted and made from a single layer of fabric and those that involve folding back the garment rather than adding a separate piece. An example of this type is the shawl collar as found on a V-neck wrap-over dress or dressing gown.

Look carefully at the sketch you are going to copy. Many collars meet edge-to-edge, often at the top of the garment opening so the collar end will lie exactly on the CF or CB, but some, such as shirt collar on a band, extend beyond the garment edge. With some styles you will have a choice. For instance a polo or roll collar can be overlapped and fastened or it can meet edge-to-edge. Other features can include such things as rouleau loops in the collar end, tucks, embroidery or other decoration which should be worked before the collar is made up.

A very important factor in achieving a neat professional-looking collar is correct choice and use of interfacing. It is as much a mistake to make a collar too stiff as to leave it too soft but, on the other hand, clever use of interfacing can enable you to use a soft fabric for a stiff style of collar if that is the fabric you want to use. Most collars are double fabric. Those with a shaped outer edge have to have a seam along the edge but straight ones such as tie collars can be made from one piece of fabric that is folded along its outer edge. A straight collar of this type is often cut on the bias so that it will give a little and fold attractively. If you wish to experiment, cut out the collar shape in soft Vilene/Pellon or an odd piece of fabric, without seam allowances and pin it on the garment or on your dummy. After adjusting it, use that as a guide and cut the collar pattern, adding seam allowances. It is always useful to check the grade of interfacing you propose to use by attaching some to a trial collar cut from the garment fabric and pin that to the garment. With most styles it will not be necessary to cut out an entire trial collar, just make half. A change of collar can often update a garment, particularly a plain or classic dress or blouse so keep any left-over fabric pieces for a possible future new collar. Needless to

say, bought clothes can also be updated with new collars made from contrasting fabric.

The main points to understand about collar shapes and the way that they sit around the neck are as follows:

1. The neckline of the garment can be one of several shapes, for example: basic, round, low round, V, square etc. This must be established before you begin to cut the collar although the neckline can, of course, be altered on the pattern if the trial collar is not satisfactory.

2. The neck edge of the collar pattern can also be one of several shapes. It can be curved like the neckline; it can be slightly curved, straight, or even slightly curved the other way, away from the neck edge. It is the relationship between the shapes of the two edges to be joined that affect what could be called the 'set' of the collar and what is known as the 'stand'. A collar with a neck edge that is similar in shape to that of the garment, will, after being attached, lie flat on the garment. A collar with less of a curve will rise slightly before folding over and lying on the garment. A collar with a straight edge will rise vertically before it folds over; the effect being to stand up loosely around the neck. A collar with an edge curving the other way will stand up and fit closely round the neck before it folds over. It is interesting to experiment with a piece of paper round the neck of the dummy in order to understand the principle.

The amount by which the collar rises is known as the 'stand'; in tailored clothes there is actually a fold line established which is stitched to emphasise it so that the collar always sits in the same position.

The part of the collar that folds over and is visible is known as the 'fall'. In classic styles, such as shirts and tailored jackets the fall is a specific amount; it is just sufficient to cover the seam that joins the collar to the garment, so it is a little more than twice the depth of the stand. A collar with stand is necessary if a tie, ribbon etc., is to go round under it ie., shirt collar.

3. The length of the neck edge of the collar pattern must equal the length of the neck edge of the garment, excluding an allowance for fastening or overlapping. With some collars the edge can be a little longer to allow the collar to be eased on, this ease should be arranged near the shoulder seams. If it is put incorrectly at the back of the neck the collar will fall outwards, away from the body.

4. The outer edge of the collar is the same length as the neckline only for a high roll collar. In fact because this type of collar is cut on the cross the outer edge actually becomes longer once it is attached. With all other collars the outer edge must be longer, considerably longer with some styles, than the neck edge of the garment. It is the difference in length between collar and outer edge and neck edge that makes it 'set'.

5. Finally, as previously stated, the outer edge of the collar can be any shape you wish. It is the combination of this and point (4) above that gives the collar its fashion point.

Flat Collars

All these collars are made using the bodice block from which to obtain the neckline shape.

(a) PETER PAN COLLAR

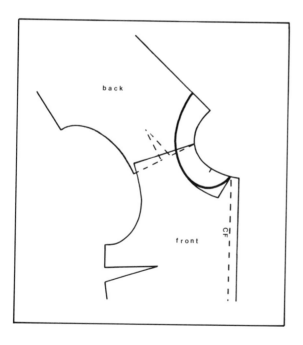

This is referred to as flat although a completely flat collar is very unattractive and allows the neck seam to show, so a small amount of stand is created by reducing the length of the outer edge a little. The Peter Pan collar may be made in one piece with the curved edges meeting at the front or in two halves if the garment opening is at the back.

Outline front bodice block as far as just below armhole. Place back bodice block against it with neck points meeting and shoulder edges together, then overlap the shoulder edges by 2cm ($\frac{3}{4}$in) **at shoulder edge only**, keeping neck points together. Outline back block to below armhole. Mark SG parallel with CB.

If there is a shoulder dart in the back bodice it is ignored for this collar. If the dart has been moved to the neckline for a better fit, it should be folded out of the block before you outline the neck. Draw the shape of the outer edge of the collar parallel with the neck edge. The width of the collar is a matter of choice; measure one on an existing garment if in doubt. Curve the collar at CF. Mark balance mark at neck and also mark position of shoulder seam on collar. Mark FOLD at CB

edge. Trace off the collar outline, cut it out and re-draw on fresh paper adding seam allowances. Label the pattern, transfer balance marks and CB fold; mark pattern CUT 2; CUT 1 in interfacing.

Notes

1. Overlapping the shoulder edges of the block creates a slight stand at the back of the neck which reduces to nothing at the CF edge. This also makes the collar slightly deeper at the front when it is attached, which is correct. If the collar is cut quite flat for some reason, ie., without any stand, it should be drawn slightly narrower round the back otherwise it will look unbalanced.

2. To cut the collar in two pieces simply curve the CB edge as well as CF. Mark SG on collar in same direction as on back block. Trace off the collar, re-cut on fresh paper adding seam allowances. Mark balance marks and also mark CB as it is difficult to distinguish between the back and the front. Mark collar CUT 4; CUT 2 in interfacing.

3. If you wish to have a gap between collar ends at CF, perhaps to make room for a bow or decorative button or if a frill or ruffle is to be inserted in the collar, draw the collar a little shorter.

4. This style of collar is usually used on softly styled clothes such as dresses and children's clothes so a soft iron-on Vilene/Pellon should be used such as Ultra-Soft or Soft, pressed to the under collar piece only.

5. Attach to neckline using bias strip or facings.

(b) FLAT COLLAR WITH STAND

The Eton-type collar

Similar to a Peter Pan collar but with a slight stand all round, this is often used on boys' shirts and on blouses. It would allow for a ribbon tie underneath.

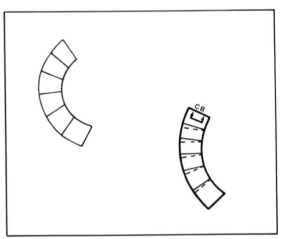

Outline the back and front bodice as for the flat collar above. Draw the collar shape required and trace off. Fold collar into 6 then fold out small darts at outer edge only on each crease or cut along each line almost to the neck edge and overlap at outer edge. Take no more than 3mm ($\frac{1}{8}$in) at each position. Shape CF edge, usually pointed on this style of collar. Outline collar on fresh paper adding seam allowances. Mark CB FOLD and mark it CUT 2; CUT 1 in interfacing.

Notes

1. This collar would normally be crisper than a flat one. Attach Soft or Ultra-Soft Vilene/Pellon to under collar, with possibly an extra piece at the corners.

2. Attach to neckline using bias strip or facings.

(c) SHAPED NECKLINE FLAT COLLAR

Sailor or Puritan collar

This method applies to many collars, the outer edge may be round, straight, scalloped etc. The illustration shows edges meeting at CF but the opening could be at the back.

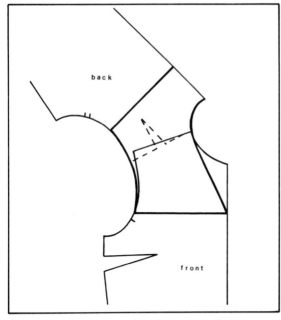

Outline front and back block as described for flat collar above. Draw a new neckline on the block. The illustration shows a V at the front but for a different style it could be V at the back, a lower round neck etc. Draw the shape of the outer edge of the collar on the front block and also on the back, trying to

ensure that the proportions are good. The back would normally be less deep to prevent it hanging out from the body over the shoulder blades. Draw the remaining collar edge over the shoulder. The illustration shows the collar the same width as the back bodice but a little wider at the shoulder seam but it could equally well be wider or narrower and a completely different shape.

Trace off the collar, marking the balance mark and shoulder seam as before and CB fold. Re-cut on fresh paper adding seam allowances. Mark it CUT 2; CUT 1 in interfacing.

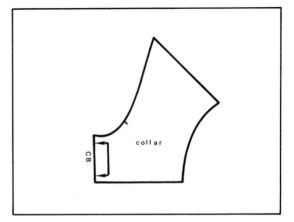

Note

This collar may require a medium-weight Vilene/Pellon, attached to under collar. Alternatively use two layers of Ultra-Soft Vilene/Pellon. Attach using bias strip at back neck to avoid bulk. Large collars are often made detachable in white or contrast fabrics. If the garment has a front opening, add the extension to CF edge after designing and tracing off the collar so that the neckline is established first.

(d) FLAT COLLAR WITH LENGTHENED OUTER EDGE

Fluted collar

This is made on the same principle as the previous collars, taking the neckline shape from the block. Outline front and back bodice blocks as before and draw in a new neckline.

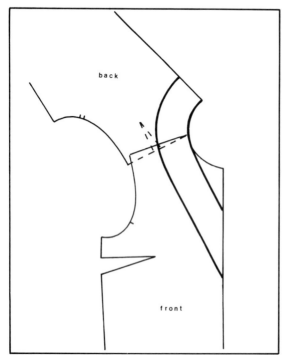

The illustration shows a V neck at CF but it could equally well be a V at the back, or both, or a low round neck etc. Draw the outer edge of the collar; this may be narrower or wider than the shoulders. Mark a balance mark on the neckline.

Trace off collar, transfer balance mark and shoulder seam. Re-cut on fresh paper. Add the balance mark and shoulder seam point; mark CB and draw SG arrow at CB edge.

Divide the collar into 6 sections, cut along each line almost to the neck edge. Spread out the collar on fresh paper and insert extra space between sections. Insert as much as you wish; the piece can finish up almost circular.

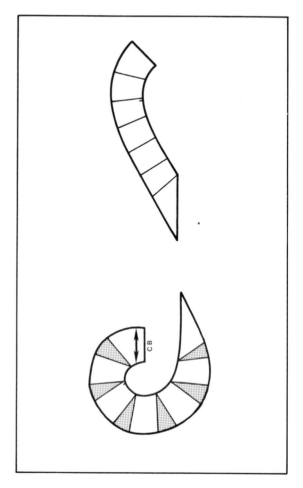

Outline the collar, add seam allowances, mark balance marks and CB, SG. Mark collar CUT 2 for a simple fluted collar, CUT 4 if you wish to make it double. There is a seam at CB.

Notes

1. Do not interface unless it is required to be stiff.

2. If more fullness is needed spread out the pieces as described and outline and cut the collar but then cut that piece in half, divide each into 6 sections and spread both halves to form a circle. Such a collar would be made from single fabric and would have 3 joins.

3. Attach to garment using bias strip.

Stand and Roll Collars

These are collars where the neck edge and outer edge are the same, or nearly the same, in length. They can be made from a rectangle. The collars stand up against the neck and are not required to sit over the shoulders, nor has the neckline to be shaped to match the garment. The bodice block could still be used, tracing off a section to the depth required and then reducing the outer edge until it equals the length of the neck edge, but this would result in a rectangle so you simply save time by starting with the rectangle.

(a) STRAIGHT STAND COLLAR

Stand-away collar

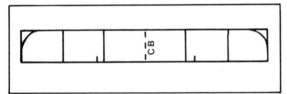

Carefully measure the neck edge of the block after adapting the neckline. Stand a tape measure on edge and measure from CF to shoulder and from CB to shoulder, excluding any dart. Draw a rectangle double that length and 3–5cm ($1\frac{1}{4}$–2in) in depth or whatever depth you wish. Add seam allowances, mark shoulder points, mark centre and label it CB; label one edge NECK EDGE and the other OUTER EDGE. Although this pattern can be cut on the straight grain it is usually only successful if the bodice neckline is lowered so that the collar stands away from the neck. A better result is obtained if it is cut on the cross. Mark SG appropriately; mark collar CUT 2; CUT 1 in interfacing. Use soft or medium iron-on Vilene/Pellon, adding a second layer if necessary.

(b) SHAPED STAND

Mandarin collar

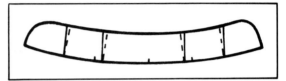

Cut a rectangle in the same way as described under (a) above. Cut out the shape and fold it in half, curve the CF ends. Fold the collar again to divide it into 6 or 8 sections. Open it out and take out tiny darts in the upper edge (outer edge of collar). Alternatively cut on each crease almost to the lower edge and overlap pieces. Do not reduce it on the centre line. You can see that this shortens the upper edge of the collar to make it hug the neck but the neck edge remains unaltered. The amount you take out can vary; it should not be more than 5mm ($\frac{1}{4}$in), and if the collar is deep, less than that. Remember the upper edge fits under the chin.

Re-draw the collar with smooth edges, adding seam allowances. Mark SG on centre crease and CF on front curved edges; mark collar CUT 2; CUT 1 in interfacing. Use soft or medium iron-on Vilene/Pellon to ensure that the collar stands up well.

Notes

1. If you propose to insert a frill or ruffle in the outer edge remember to include its depth when you decide on the collar depth. Also, allow for the frill or ruffle at the CF. You may want the frill or ruffle edges to meet edge-to-edge. Alternatively if there is to be an extension for buttons on the bodice it looks quite nice if the collar edges meet but the frills or ruffles overlap.

2. You may want this collar to overlap and fasten, in which case adapt the front bodice to

include the extra needed for the fastening and then measure the neckline of the adapted block to ascertain the length of the collar rectangle.

(c) STRAIGHT BIAS COLLAR

Polo or Roll collar

This collar is usually fairly wide so that it rolls over. It can be attached to a high or slightly scooped out neckline. Alternatively the neckline can be lowered at front or back and the collar then falls into a cowl. The collar is cut on the bias so that the outer edge gives, although, when using soft jersey, it can be cut on the straight grain.

Adapt bodice neckline if necessary. Measure length of neck edge on bodice block, ignoring any back dart. Draw a rectangle double that length and the width you need. Calculate the width as four times the depth you want the finished collar. Mark shoulder points and CF by measuring the collar pattern carefully against the block. Fold pattern at right angles to find SG line on the cross. Cut out adding seam allowances. Mark collar CUT 1.

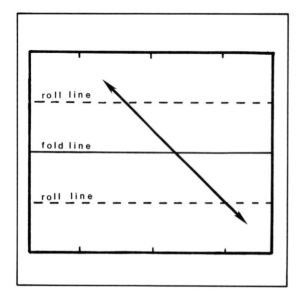

Notes

1. If attached to a lowered neckline the collar ends can be joined to eliminate an opening.

2. If an opening is necessary fasten the collar edge to edge with Velcro or hooks. Alternatively if the garment has a zipper (CF or CB) you can take the zipper into the collar to fasten it, either half-way or right to the top of the collar.

3. In a soft fabric or for a cowl effect make the collar 2cm ($\frac{3}{4}$in) longer than the neck edge and ease the surplus into the neckline at the shoulder seam points. The ease has the effect of providing a longer outer edge to the collar.

4. Interfacing should not be used across the entire collar as it prevents it from falling correctly. In woven fabrics a narrow strip of soft iron-on Vilene/Pellon can be attached to the neck edge, to reinforce the neck join, but in jersey fabrics omit interfacing altogether, inserting a length of bias tape in the neck seam instead.

(d) STRAIGHT BIAS COLLAR WITH TIE ENDS

This is probably the easiest collar to construct because the fit of the neckline is not crucial because the tie can be used to slightly tighten or loosen it. Also the length does not have to be calculated quite so accurately. The bias collar can be narrow or wide, the ends can be long for a bow or short for a loop-over and it can be made in almost any fabric.

The neckline of the bodice can be high and round, as on the block, in which case the garment would need an opening at CB or CF and a break in the collar; or the neckline can be low and round, boat-shaped or V. This is a good collar for a side fastened bodice too.

Adjust the block neckline appropriately and measure the total length of back and front, ignoring any dart. Cut a rectangle twice that length and twice the depth required, remembering that the collar will be soft and will wrinkle or even fold over. Mark CB, and shoulder seam points from block and CF points. Extend the pattern each end by the amount you will require to tie it. Add seam allowances and cut out. Fold pattern at right angles and mark SG on bias. It is quite likely that the collar will have to be cut in two pieces if fabric is narrow or for economy, so draw a line on the straight grain in the middle to indicate where to cut the pattern if necessary. Mark pattern CUT 1, although if a join is needed you could cut the pattern and place one piece on double fabric to cut out.

garment will be stitched to the facing from the dot to the front edge and down to the hem; it is then turned RS out leaving the neck edge free to be stitched to the'collar. If there is no CF opening, snip the fabric in as far as the dot on the bodice, fold in to the WS the small 2cm ($\frac{3}{4}$in) long edge and secure to the garment – a small piece of Wundaweb/Stitch Witchery/Save-a-Stitch is the most satisfactory method of doing this. This leaves the neck edge free for attaching to the collar.

2. If the garment opening is at CB the collar must be cut in two pieces with the CB ends

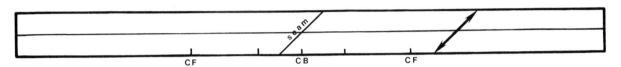

CF   CB   CF

Notes

1. Measure 1cm ($\frac{3}{8}$ in) within CF points and put a dot near the edge of the pattern. These are the points to stitch to when attaching collar to neckline. It leaves a gap between the ends so that the knot can be tied. Mark dots to correspond on the bodice pattern 1cm ($\frac{3}{8}$ in) inside the CF line. If there is a CF opening, the

straight. After stitching across ends and turning collar RS out they can be fastened edge-to-edge with Velcro or hooks, or if the garment has a zipper, it can be taken up into the collar.

3. If the garment has an assymmetrical fastening, adjust the length of each tie end accordingly: CF, CB and stitching dots are even more important in this case.

Stand and Fall Collars

These are those which have a longer outer edge but which have a neck edge shaped in the opposite direction to the curve of the neckline. The collar is folded round the neck, part of it hugging the neck in a stand, the other part falling over and covering the stand.

(a) POINTED COLLAR

This is the type often used on a blouse or, as a slightly different shape, on a coat or jacket.

The garment has a front opening which can be fastened to the neck bringing the collar edges together, or it can be open at the neck, the facings on the garment forming revers or lapels. It is also known as a convertible collar for this reason.

Measure neck edge of front and back bodice block ignoring any dart. Draw a rectangle that length and 7–9cm (2$\frac{3}{4}$in–3$\frac{1}{2}$in) deep. Mark one end CB FOLD; mark shoulder seam point. Half-way between shoulder and CF end start to curve the lower edge, neck edge, of collar up to a point 1cm ($\frac{3}{8}$in) above the line at CF. This is the shaping to create the 'stand' across the back of the neck. Lengthen the other edge, by 1.5cm ($\frac{5}{8}$in) to produce a better collar point and rule a line from that point back to CF line, to meet the end of the curved neck edge. Cut out adding seam allowances. Mark collar CUT 2 to FOLD; CUT 1 in interfacing. Use soft or medium iron-on Vilene/Pellon, adding a second piece if necessary to the collar points.

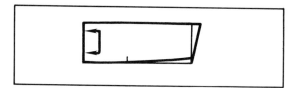

Note

The outer edge of the collar is straight and could be a fold instead of a seam. Place on a folded piece of paper with outer edge on fold and re-cut adding seam allowances to the end and the neck edge. Open out and mark it CUT 1 to FOLD. Do not interface the entire collar but use sew-in Vilene/Pellon as far as the middle only, attaching the free edge to the fabric with catch stitch. This part is the under collar.

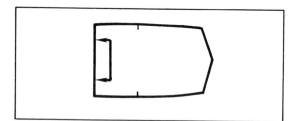

(b) COLLAR WITH SHAPED POINTS

Depending on fashion, the collar can be curved to form a collar with round 'city-style' ends – this should be well stiffened with interfacing, or, shaped, longer points can be added, even wide rounded ends can be drawn. In each case take the shaping from mid-way between

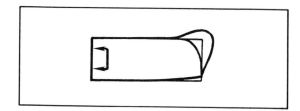

shoulder and CF, and draw the outer edge as you wish. Mark it CB FOLD at the other end, and label it CUT 2 to FOLD; CUT 1 in interfacing. It will now have a seam along the outer edge. Use soft or medium iron-on Vilene/Pellon on the under collar with additional pieces at the ends for extra stiffness.

Note

These collars may have frills or ruffles inserted in outer edge but rather than shorten the collar at CF end it would look better to taper the frill or ruffle to nothing by the time it reaches the neck edge.

(c) SHIRT COLLAR

This collar is more shaped than (a) or (b) so that it fits the neck closely, stands up higher and also allows for a tie if necessary.

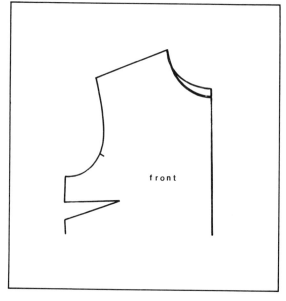

front

Begin by lowering the front neckline by 1.5cm ($\frac{5}{8}$in) at CF. Measure length of neck edge of back and front bodice, ignoring any darts. Draw a rectangle that length and 10cm (4in) deep. Mark shoulder same position, mark CB FOLD at one end. Rule a line across the rectangle half-way between shoulder point and CF. Measure 3cm (1$\frac{1}{4}$in) up from neck edge at CF and draw the collar point and outer edge as you wish. On the neck edge curve edge up from the guide line towards the CF but continue beyond CF for 2cm ($\frac{3}{4}$in). Curve from that point round to the CF line. This extension is for the top button. The end of the extension must finish level with the button extension on the garment when attached. If you want a wider or narrower button-over extension on the garment then the collar extension must be adjusted.

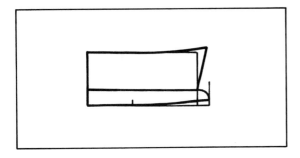

Re-cut the pattern adding seam allowances. Mark it CUT 2 to FOLD; CUT 1 in interfacing. Use soft or medium iron-on Vilene/Pellon attached to under collar adding extra pieces at the points and along the neck edge if you wish.

(d) SHIRT COLLAR WITH BAND

A collar that fits even more closely and has an even better shape is made by cutting the 'rise' part – the stand, separately from the 'fall' part. The closer fit is achieved by removing a section of pattern between the stand and the fall and creating a shaped seam.

Make collar pattern as described for (c) above, mark a balance mark at the guide line and cut off the stand. This becomes the collar band. Re-cut on a folded piece of paper. Mark it CUT 2; CUT 1 in interfacing.

Trim 1cm ($\frac{3}{8}$ in) from collar at CB end, curving it gradually to nothing at the construction line point. Re-cut the collar on a folded piece of paper to make a complete pattern piece.

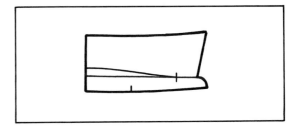

Open it out and mark it CUT 2; 1 in interfacing. Mark CB on both collar and band and also the balance marks. Mark SG as shown although both can be turned round if you want a particular effect in patterned fabric. A good tip when interfacing is to use a soft variety in the main part but a crisper one, two layers of the soft one, on the collar band. In addition extra pieces can be added to the collar points if necessary.

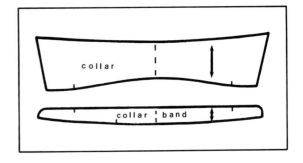

Frills and Ruffles

Frills or ruffles can be added anywhere, at garment edges or within a garment section. If you can arrange to have a seam at the point where you want the frill or ruffle, it is easy to enclose the raw edges with seam stitching. If there is no seam the frill or ruffle must be applied to RS and in this case allow for it to have a heading ie., a small amount to stand up above the gathering thread. When stitching it, both edges of the frill or ruffle are hemmed and the frill or ruffle attached by placing it on the RS and stitching on the gathering line.

The frill or ruffle is a straight piece of fabric cut to the depth you require plus seam allowances. You need not necessarily cut the pattern pieces unless you need them in order to calculate the fabric quantity. Decide on the depth of the frill or ruffle having regard to the position on the garment and the proportions of the area of garment to which they will be attached. Narrow frills or ruffles are easier to make if they are cut double width and have a fold at the outer edge instead of a hem.

When calculating the length of a frill or ruffle allow $1\frac{1}{2}$ times the length of the garment edge, or twice the amount in fine fabric, for a full frill or ruffle. Remember that the exact amount is not crucial: if it fits better on the fabric it will not matter if it is a little shorter or longer. You can economise on fabric by allowing 1cm ($\frac{3}{8}$in) seam allowances, or even less, for hems and joins. Mark the amount on the pattern as a reminder.

To add frills or ruffles in the middle of a garment piece, draw a line on the pattern in frill or ruffle position on front, or on back and front. Mark balance marks across the line, cut the pattern and outline the pieces, again adding seam allowances.

Notes

1. If there is shaping nearby eg., bust dart, this can be moved into the seam made for the frill or ruffle. See section on yokes page 72ff.

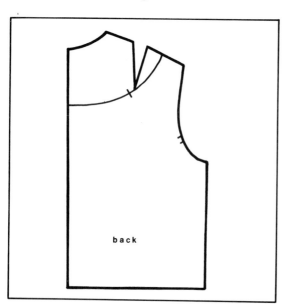

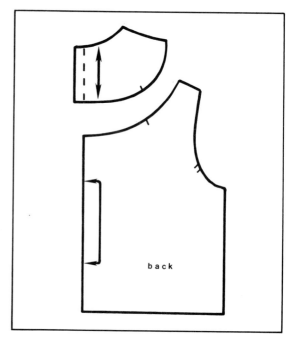

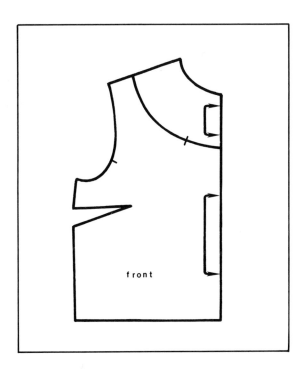

2. The most accurate way of re-joining the seam is to pin the made frill or ruffle to RS of larger piece of garment, gathering it to fit. Baste in place and machine it. Remove gathering threads to soften the seam, place second garment piece on top RS down, matching balance marks and edges, and baste. To stitch the seam turn the garment over and follow the first line of stitching.

3. Ends of frills or ruffles look neat if inserted into seam eg., shoulder seam, but remember that they are difficult to iron after laundering.

4. When adding a frill or ruffle all round a garment eg., skirt, make all the joins in frill or ruffle and in garment, divide both into 4 or 6 and attach frill or ruffle.

Pockets

Pockets can be functional, decorative or both. The decision as to size and position depends on the style of the garment. The decision about position relates to whether or not it will be used. It is easy to make mistakes. For instance sports clothes must always have a pocket but a small shaped pocket on the bust of a T-shirt cannot be used especially if door keys and plasters have to be carried in addition to a handkerchief. Equally, a large back or front patch pocket will not do: things will jump out. Very large pockets may look right but things obviously settle in the bottom and are difficult to reach.

A pocket is a bag that is formed either by placing a piece of fabric on the outside of the garment ie., patch pocket, or by making a bag from two layers of fabric to hang inside the garment. With the second type it can be joined to an existing seam and be well concealed, or where there is no convenient seam, the garment has to be cut and edges finished with a binding, welt, flap etc. A decorative pocket is usually a patch pocket of any shape, colour, position; a flap or a welt can be added to classic coats etc., simply to break up an area without actually cutting the garment or adding the bag.

Decide on the type of pocket you think might be suitable, bearing in mind the amount of fabric there may be, then cut the proposed pattern shape and place it on the garment pattern, moving it and adjusting its size if necessary. Mark the final position on the pat-

tern. If you do not want to make a final decision, wait until the garment is ready to be
fitted and cut a pocket pattern from Vilene/
Pellon and pin it to the garment to establish
the size and position.

Opening	13–15cm	(5–6in)
	8–12cm	$(3\frac{1}{4}$–$4\frac{3}{4}$in)
	14–18cm	$(5\frac{1}{2}$–7in)
Depth	15–23cm	(6–9in)
	9–13cm	$(3\frac{1}{2}$–5in)
	17–26cm	$(6\frac{1}{2}$–$10\frac{1}{4}$in)

(a) PATCH POCKETS

These can be single, double or lined and
used on any garment. Single fabric pockets
need a wide hem at the open side which can
be stitched or left loose. Remember that
lightweight Fold-a-Band/Fuse'n'Fold/Waist-
Shaper pressed to the WS not only gives you
a reinforced edge but also a fold line. Add
a hem allowance of 3cm $(1\frac{1}{4}$in) for Fold-a-
band/Fuse'n'Fold/Waist-Shaper. Large patch

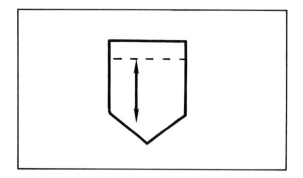

pockets should be completely backed with
light iron-on Vilene/Pellon so that they do
not gape. Cut out pockets that are angled or
curved from a piece of folded paper for accuracy. On all edges except the opening a narrow seam allowance of 1cm $(\frac{3}{8}$in) is sufficient
and on shaped pockets this makes it easier
to handle them, but remember to mark the
pattern edge appropriately as a reminder.
Square or pointed pockets can also have a

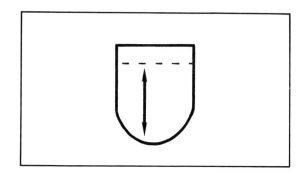

fold-over flap or a separate flap to button
down. Remember that Fold-a-Band/Fuse'n'-
Fold/Waist shaper is a useful aid here too. If
any decoration such as tucks, ribbon, etc., is
to be put on the pocket, work it on a large
piece of fabric then fold it and pin on the
pattern to cut out to size. To cut a safari-style
pleated pocket fold the pleat in a piece of
paper, then draw the pocket outline.

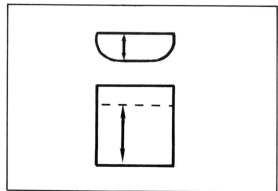

Rule the SG arrow vertically, outline pattern or, if it is to be cut on the cross in check or
striped fabric, mark it at 45 degrees. Label
pattern CUT 1, CUT 2 etc. Mark pocket positions on RS garment fabric by the most convenient method. If applying one pocket only
mark the position of the top corners using
fabric pen, tailor's chalk or a line of basting.
Use tailor basting if a pair of pockets is to be
attached, folding the fabric evenly first. An
alternative and very satisfactory method is to
mark the position on RS with tailor's chalk,
fold fabric evenly RS inside or place second

piece on top RS down, bang down sharply with your hand and you will find two clear marks on the corresponding pieces. Attach patch pockets to garment as easily as possible in construction so that fabric can be held flat; this is especially important on full or gathered styles.

(b) SEAM POCKETS

Mainly used in skirts, trousers and dresses. They are made from two hand-shaped pieces of fabric or lining with one edge straight and equal in length to the required opening. Note that if the hand is to go in at an angle, as it will if the pocket is in a vertical seam, the opening should be longer than on a horizontal pocket.

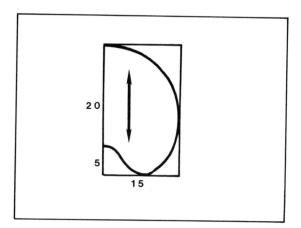

Draw the pocket pattern as shown and add seam allowances; cut two for each pocket. Mark a balance mark or a notch on the straight edge and a corresponding mark on the seam edges to which it will join. Note that this pattern shape, before seam allowances are added can, if the fabric is wide enough, be placed against the garment edge and the whole piece cut as one with the pocket as an extension. To make up, stitch garment seam to 1.5cm ($\frac{5}{8}$in) inside pocket, turn and stitch round outer edges of pocket bag, turn again and complete garment seam. Snip one seam

allowance at top and bottom of pocket so that it can be pressed towards the front.

You can ensure that this type of pocket lies flat in wear and does not cause a bulky ridge by pressing light iron-on Vilene/Pellon to WS of one piece when cutting out. Alternatively stitch one end of a piece tape to the upper edge of the bag and include the other end in with the waistband stitching.

(c) INSET POCKET

Used a great deal on trousers and shorts and sometimes skirts, this pocket is really a combination of a seam pocket, cut pocket and patch pocket. Although the bag hangs inside the garment, the opening for the hand is stitched in with the waist and the side seam. The opening edge can be straight or curved. It is a particularly slimming feature.

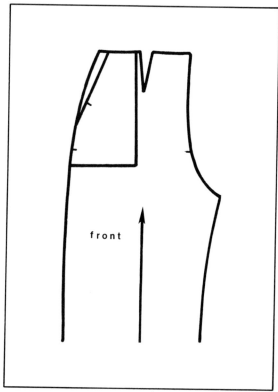

Outline the trouser block. Draw the pocket opening between waist and side seam. Keep it to about 12–14cm ($4\frac{3}{4}$–$5\frac{1}{2}$in) long; if it is too long the pocket will gape. Draw the shape of the pocket bag which should be about 24cm ($9\frac{1}{2}$in) deep from the waist and 13cm (5in) wide. The bottom corner of the bag can be curved if you wish. Trace off the bag shape including pocket opening edge, adding two balance marks as shown. Mark SG and label it

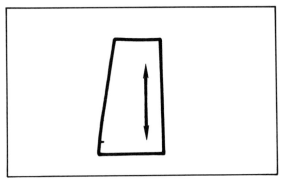

POCKET BAG FACING: Cut 1 for each pocket. Trace off the bag shape again but this time following the outer edge of the trouser. Mark SG and label it SIDE SECTION: Cut 1 for each pocket. Add balance mark. Finally trim off the trouser along the pocket opening line. Mark balance marks, add SG and mark it TROUSER FRONT. Cut 2. Add seam allowances to all pieces.

To construct the pocket interface opening edge, stitch pocket bag facing to front trouser with RS together and stitch along pocket opening edge. Roll facing to WS, press edge

and top stitch. Place trouser leg RS up on RS of side section, matching balance marks; baste in position and secure by machining along the waist and side seam edges 1cm ($\frac{3}{8}$in) from the edge. Stitch bag pieces together round outer edge.

Notes

1. To reduce bulk the pocket bag facing can be made from lining or thin cotton.

2. If you prefer a side zipper it should be short enough to avoid the pocket.

3. Darts and tucks should be put in after attaching bag facing piece but before attaching to a side section.

4. In a full skirt this pocket can conceal a wrap opening, so dispensing with a zipper. To do this do not stitch edges together along waist; instead, complete skirt and attach waistband arranging it so that it extends to the pocket edges on outer and inner layer to form the wrap-over for fastening. Complete the waistband. Join pocket bag edges round lower edge only leaving 15cm (6in) open below waist.

Tucks

Allowance for tucks can be added wherever you wish on a pattern piece but avoid areas with darts and keep them on the SG or they are difficult to stitch flat. They can be decorative ie., stitched for their entire length, or functional and stitched only part of the way. Examples of this second type include tucks in the top or wrist of a sleeve or at the shoulder or waist of a bodice. For these kinds you must insert additional width all down the pattern piece but draw the stitching lines for the tuck to the correct length.

For tucks to be stitched flat you can rule parallel lines for each tuck on the pattern then transfer the lines to the fabric with tailor tacks. But if you intend to make pin-tucks or lines of twin needle stitching, you will find it difficult to do it this way accurately. The solution is to mark a few parallel lines, or perhaps two lines marking a section to be tucked without enlarging the pattern and work the stitching you need on a piece of fabric before pinning on the pattern and cutting out.

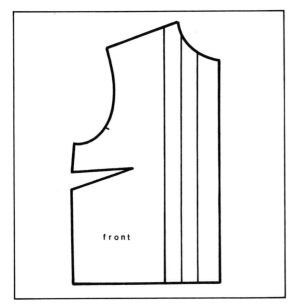

To insert extra in the pattern for wide tucks, draw a line to mark the first one, either centrally on the pattern piece or parallel with CF, and draw other lines for more tucks parallel with the first. Pin the side of the pattern to new paper and cut on one line at a time spreading the pieces each time and inserting an even amount before pinning again. Be sure to keep the pieces on one level. Draw the tucks on the paper beneath and cut along the edges that are not affected by tucks; add seam allowances. Fold the tucks into the paper and flatten them in the correct direction then cut along pattern edge, adding seam allowances. Open out the pattern, label it and mark SG lines.

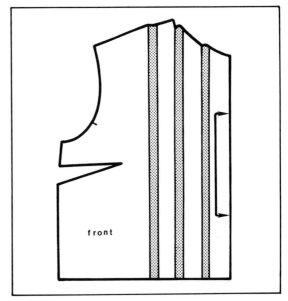

Notes

1. A good finish can be achieved on wide flat tucks in medium-weight fabrics by pressing soft Fold-a-Band/Fuse'n'Fold/Waist-Shaper to WS of fabric before folding and stitching. Not only does this reinforce the

tuck, it also makes a crisp fold. Insert the correct amount of extra paper for each ie., 6cm ($2\frac{1}{2}$ in) the width of Fold-a-Band/Fuse'n'Fold/Waist-Shaper.

2. The easiest way to mark flat tucks on the fabric is to tailor tack through both layers, folding the paper back along each line in turn. However, a further tip is to mark the centre, or fold, of each tuck and one stitching line, then to stitch them, fold the fabric along the centre of the tuck, press, baste and stitch on the marked stitching line. Press the tuck, make the next one and so on.

3. The easiest way to stitch pin tucks is to fold the fabric WS together, on the SG, exactly where the first tuck is to be, press the fold and stitch immediately. No basting is necessary. Set your adjustable marker to the required distance, measure and fold for the next tuck, press and stitch, and so on.

4. The easiest way to make twin-needle tucks is to make the first tuck in position on the SG, marking dots with fabric pen or tailor's chalk if the grain is difficult to follow. Subsequent tucks are made, keeping them parallel, by using the edge of the foot as a space guide, or for close tucks, by fitting the previous tuck into the groove on the under side of the foot. Press tuck on WS only.

Waistbands

There are several ways of making a pattern for a waistband. There are also ways of making it directly in fabric and dispensing with the pattern although if it is to be stored for future use it is probably more sensible to make the complete pattern for the garment.

STRAIGHT WAISTBAND

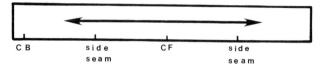

The depth of the pattern must be twice that of the stiffening you select. Many types of waistbanding, petersham etc., are 2.5cm (1in) wide but if you plan to have a wider band, or perhaps a narrower one, buy the stiffening before making the pattern. Draw a rectangle on pattern paper: waist measurement plus 2.5cm (1in) wide ease in length and twice the width of the stiffening plus 1.5cm ($\frac{5}{8}$in) all round for seam allowances. Mark the centre and quarter points. If the skirt or trousers are to fasten at the left side, mark the centre point SIDE SEAM, and the other two CENTRE FRONT and CENTRE BACK. If the garment is to fasten at the back the centre mark is the CENTRE FRONT, the others are SIDE SEAM points. If the garment is to fasten at the front the centre mark is the CENTRE BACK and the others SIDE SEAM points. Mark the pattern appropriately. Draw a straight grain arrow along the middle although your fabric may require you to cut it the other way. Finally add the extension for wrap-over. The amount you add will depend on how you intend fastening the garment. Add: 4cm ($1\frac{1}{2}$in) for 1 hook and 1 press stud; 3cm ($1\frac{1}{4}$in) for a button and a buttonhole; 6cm ($2\frac{1}{2}$in) or more for Velcro.

If you cannot decide at this stage, add the maximum and trim it later if necessary. Mark the pattern CUT 1.

CURVED WAISTBAND

This should be no wider than 2.5cm (1in), the upper edge being the waistline. Stiffen the waistband with curved petersham; buy it beforehand and use it to obtain the shape of the pattern. Cut the petersham to waist size plus a short extension for fastening. Outline the petersham on pattern paper, add a seam allowance of 1.5cm ($\frac{5}{8}$in) all round. Draw a straight grain arrow across the middle, mark the centre and quarters, remembering to exclude the extension. Mark the pattern CUT 2 as the waistband is made with a seam along the upper edge. If using bulky fabric cut the inner piece from lining fabric. The lower edge of the waistband is slightly longer and settles below the natural waist. When making the garment attach the waistband slightly below the marked waistline.

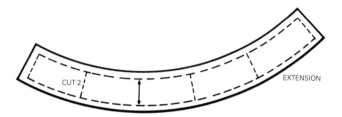

FOLD-A-BAND/FUSE'N'FOLD/ WAIST-SHAPERWAISTBAND

The easiest way to use Fold-a-Band/Fuse'n' Fold/Waist-Shaper to stiffen a waistband is to dispense with a pattern, put it round your waist, add extra for the extension, cut it and simply place it on the WS of the fabric matching the central perforations to the straight grain and press. Cut out round the outer edge and attach to the garment. Remember that the perforations along the sides represent the stitching line: the seam allowance is 1cm ($\frac{3}{8}$in).

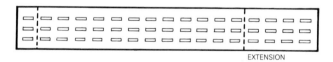

WRAP-OVER SKIRT WAISTBAND

Cut the pattern to the appropriate width as described above but make it exactly the same length as the waist of the skirt pattern. To do this accurately measure and mark off along the edge of a piece of pattern paper, along the waistline, not the pattern edge, of the back and the front skirt. Remember to exclude the darts and side and centre seam allowances. Double the length of the measured piece to bring it to full waist size and cut out the rectangle. Mark the straight grain down the middle and mark the centre and seam points.

CF   CB   CF

ELASTIC WAISTBAND

This is a useful waist finish on lightweight or stretch trousers and gathered skirts. As it eliminates a zipper it is a method to recommend to beginners. Obtain a waistlength of suitable elastic. Conventional elastic which is thick and firm should be 1.5–2.5cm ($\frac{5}{8}$–1in) wide but elastic webbing, which is open and more stretchy, can be from 2.5–7.5cm (1–3in) in width. Cut a rectangle of paper twice the width of the elastic and $1\frac{1}{2}$ times waist size in length. Add 1.5cm ($\frac{5}{8}$in) seam allowance all round. Mark the straight grain along the middle. At the ends mark the centre and also the seam line at one edge, with a dot. After cutting out the fabric fold the waistband RS together with ends level and stitch from each edge to the dot. Press open the join. Fold the band WS inside and press with raw edges level. Attach to RS skirt, gathering skirt to fit. Press band to extend above top of skirt. Thread elastic through band and join ends, slip stitch the slot in the band.

OTHER BLOCKS

HIP LENGTH BODICE BLOCK

The bodice block included with the book and which you have adjusted is for dresses and fitted tops. You will often need a longer, looser outline to use for blouses, shirts and tunics so it is worth making a hip length block in card. You will also be able to use it for simple dress patterns, by extending the centre and side seam lines.

Adjust back and front alike. Outline bodice block with CB or CF line on straight edge of paper. Put fitted skirt block against it also with CB or CF line on edge of paper but with waist edges together near that edge. The bodice will overlap. Outline skirt block down to hip level. Rule a vertical line through centre of waist dart to 12cm ($4\frac{3}{4}$in) below waist. Join ends of bodice waist dart to meet on this line to form a double-ended dart. This dart is often used on

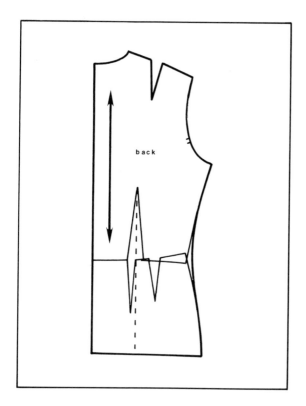

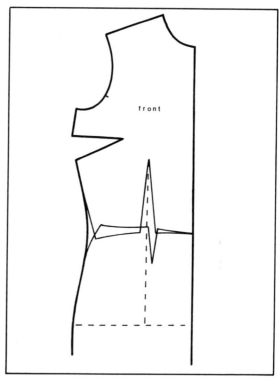

tunics, dresses and jackets, and sometimes on fitted blouses but it can be ignored for a looser fit. Draw a new waistline across the block at right angles to the CB and CF. Draw a new side seam to give a less fitted waist. Copy this block onto card, transfer balance marks.

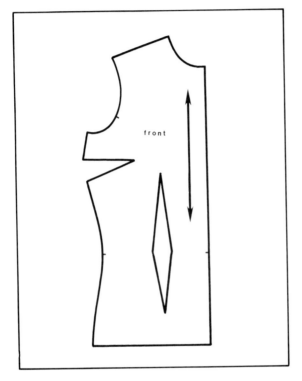

Note

Patterns cut from this block will fit around the hips in the same way as the skirt block. If you want it looser, add extra to side seams when cutting pattern. If you are doing an adaptation that includes adding extra width for gathers etc., then this is not necessary.

LOOSER FITTING BODICE BLOCK

Unless waist darts are in fashion or you usually have them for comfort or a better fit, you may find it useful to make a cardboard block of a waistlength block without darts.

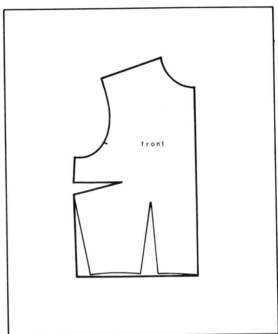

Outline the front bodice block on paper. Cut long underarm and waist dart to BP. Close underarm dart to bring side seam edge of block vertical. Outline the block like this, drawing a new side seam and waist seam. Insert balance marks and draw in the underarm dart. To make a back block, outline fitted block and rule a straight side seam to correspond with that of the front. Ignore the waist dart. Cut out both in card.

DRESS BLOCK

It is a simple matter to convert the hip length block to a one-piece dress pattern but if you wear this style of dress a lot, make a block in cardboard. Outline hip length block and extend the side seam edges to length required at the same angle. Rule a guide line from CF and CB edge at right angles but then curve the hemline. Check width of pattern at hipline, sloping line out further if necessary.

Adaptations to the above are made as described throughout the book.

Dresses

WITHOUT WAIST SEAM

These styles can hang straight from the shoulders or the waistline can be defined with a drawstring, elastic or a belt.

(a) A-LINE DRESS

Use hip length block or one-piece dress block. Extend to length required then add 6cm ($2\frac{1}{2}$in) to side edge at hem. Redraw side seams and curve hem up 1cm ($\frac{3}{8}$in) at sides. Use the underarm dart and shoulder or neck dart and use front and back double-ended waist darts only for a fitted dress.

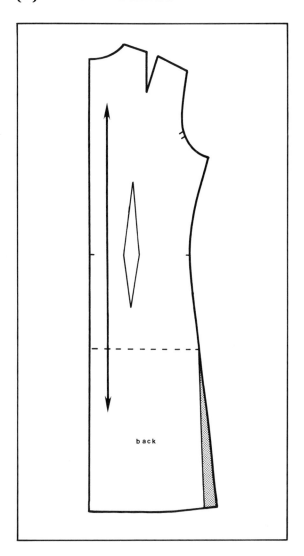

back

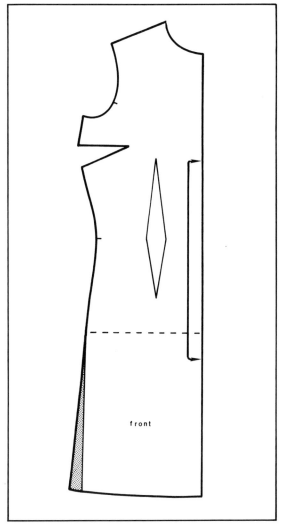

front

(b) STRAIGHT DRESS

Outline hip length block. Rule straight side seams from underarm to hem passing through hip point on block. Curve hem slightly. Use underarm and neckline dart, omit waist darts unless a sheath style is required.

Note

This pattern looks good made as a sweater dress in knits of all types and weights. You may want to make it fit more tightly by taking in the side seams.

WITH WAIST SEAM

Any full skirt can be gathered to fit any style of bodice but to make a skirt pattern to join the bodice at the waist requires some adjustments. You can also join a bodice to the trousers.

Adapt the bodice first to make the pattern then outline the A-Line skirt or trouser block along the sides. Hold it with the waist edge against the bodice waist and outline the skirt darts to original size but so that they line up with the bodice dart. Redraw darts on both slightly shorter and narrower to give a looser fit at the waist. Check that waist edges are equal in length, if they are not, add on to the smaller one.

To join trousers to bodice, adjust darts as described above, omitting one of the trouser darts. You will have a more comfortable jumpsuit if you lengthen the crotch seam a little by scooping it out. Make sure the garment opening runs from neck to crotch curve.

GENERAL INFORMATION
Calculating Fabric Quantities

It is obviously impossible to give you any idea of how much fabric you will need for a particular adaptation but it is not difficult to work it out for yourself. The only problem is that until you know what type and design of fabric you are going to use, you cannot make the pattern. Also it is much more interesting, and you will be more successful, if you design and cut the pattern for a specific fabric that you have beside you and that you can see and handle. However, to balance this there is the advantage that you will be able to use this book to make patterns that will use up some of the lengths of fabric you have had lying around for so long. There is no clear-cut solution but take note of this valuable tip. When you have made a pattern and have it pinned to the fabric, measure exactly how much you are using. Make a note of the amount and the width, attach a piece of the fabric and put it in the envelope with the pattern when you store it away. If you have a computer at home, store all your information on it, including notes on making up and how the project went.

If you have cut the pattern pieces and wish to work out how much fabric to buy, simply lay them out on an old length of material, or on your cutting board, and measure off what it takes. All pieces must of course be correctly placed to grain, fold etc., and allowance made for bias strips, frills or ruffles and the like. If you are nervous or don't trust your calculations you might like to do what commercial pattern companies do and add an extra 10% for what they term 'scissor fright'.

Do remember to add extra for matching patterns and checks: you need one extra pattern for each main piece ie., bodice, sleeve, skirt. Also, for one-way designs, pile fabric etc., the pattern pieces must be placed all facing in one direction when you are making your calculation.

If by any chance you make a mistake, rectify it with the addition of contrasts or better still, cut another style of pattern that will fit the fabric.

TRIMMINGS

To work out how much bias binding, lace, piping etc., you will need, measure all the appropriate edges. Remember to count up the number of buttons you need too.

HABERDASHERY

Ideally keep a stock of things like Fold-a-Band/Fuse'n'Fold/Waist-Shaper and Vilene/Pellon so that you can select the best type when you need it. If you can't do that measure up how much you will need and add it to your list. Buy your zipper too. As the range of lengths is limited it is sensible to get the zipper and then mark its length on the pattern rather than mark the pattern first. You will need things like Velcro and hooks too,

although again it is sensible to build up a stock.

You will need 2 reels of thread per garment, 3 if there are lots of long seams to be zig-zagged. Drima, the spun polyester thread sews on all fabrics and is essential for stretch or jersey fabrics in order to avoid seam splitting. Duet which has a fine covering of cotton, is slightly less lustrous but is strong. I find it excellent for hand-sewing and I also find less static builds up when stitching woven synthetic fabrics.

Cutting Out

If you laid out your pattern in order to calculate the quantity of fabric required you will have already worked out how to place the pattern on the fabric. It might be wise to make a rough sketch of the position of each piece to save doing it again when you have the fabric.

If you are an experienced dressmaker laying out the pieces and cutting out will hold no terror for you. For others, especially those who perhaps once made a small error in cutting out, albeit years ago, it may be an anxious time, although there is no reason for this to be so. There is no mystery about pinning the pattern to the fabric and since you have now made your own pattern and marked it FOLD, SG etc., you can see that all you have to do is follow your own markings.

First fold the fabric roughly to see if all the pieces fit across the width. If not, open out part of it flat for those pieces to be placed twice and see whether smaller pieces will fit if you fold one selvedge over for a short dis-

tance. Always place large pieces first but at the same time seeing which smaller pieces fit in between. Earmark long narrow selvedge pieces for waistbands, belts, button bands etc. If the big pieces still won't go on, see whether it works to cut them on single fabric (twice) on the whole width then refold the remainder of the length for all the smaller pieces. Remember that a long narrow piece on the fold can be opened out; it will often then take a collar, even the sleeves. The hollows from the armhole and crotch are useful for bias strips and neck facings.

If you are just a little short of fabric make pocket bags from lining; use bias strips to attach collars in place of facings; attach petersham instead of a waistband etc.

Do cut each piece on the correct grain; do place pieces to FOLD where necessary; do check that you have used all the pattern pieces and then cut out.

Interfacing

Use your dressmaking experience to guide you as to where to add interfacing. Interface all features such as collars and all fastening edges and any other area you decide should be reinforced either to withstand wear or for emphasis. It helps to decide before cutting the pattern so that the pattern is accurate. For example, soft Fold-a-Band/Fuse'n'Fold/Waist-Shaper has no seam allowance and is 3cm ($1\frac{1}{4}$in) wide on each side of the perforations. This can be used for cuffs, bands, straps, pocket tops, button edges and many other things. Firm Fold-a-Band/Fuse'n'Fold/Waist-Shaper for waistbands is available in several widths and it has 1cm ($\frac{3}{8}$ in) seam allowance on each edge. You may like to make your pattern seam allowance to match it as well as the width.

There are many iron-on and sew-in interfacings. They vary in width and some of them, even non-woven, have to be cut on the straight grain. Bear this in mind when deciding which areas to interface.

If you are reasonably experienced at sewing you will probably not need to make separate pattern pieces for interfacing. Remember to mark collars etc., with the word 'Interfacing' to remind you. Also use the same pattern piece where an edge or internal area needs interfacing, shade it on the pattern with diagonal lines or a coloured pencil to remind you when cutting out.

Lining

Commercial paper patterns often include separate pieces for cutting lining. This is not strictly necessary although there are some alterations to be made and points to remember.

1. Use the pattern and cut out the fabric first.

2. With the exception of underarm darts, back neck or shoulder darts and back darts in skirts and trousers, mark darts to be stitched as tucks 2cm ($\frac{3}{4}$in) shorter, or as folded unstitched tucks.

3. Look at the pattern and see where straight seams could become a fold in the lining etc., back skirt. Fold back seam allowance and mark edge LINING FOLD.

4. Reduce the hem allowance. The lining should be 3cm ($1\frac{1}{4}$in) shorter than the garment when finished so if you put a narrow hem on the lining you can fold back a fair amount of pattern at the hem. Label it LINING HEM.

5. Fold back any pleat extensions and cut lining so that you can stitch as a seam to the top of the pleat but leave a hemmed slit below.

6. At opening edges that are faced, mark a line on the pattern to indicate where the facing extends to (these may already exist as a perforated line) and draw a cutting line for lining 1.5cm ($\frac{5}{8}$in) outside it. Label it LINING CUTTING LINE.

7. Finally, when you cut out, add 2mm ($\frac{1}{16}$in) or so to the outer edges. Lining fabrics haven't much give and they will wear better if the lining is slightly loose inside the garment.

Adapting Commercial
Patterns

There are other designs that have been omitted from this book because they depend on specific measurements or because there are several complicated stages involved. These include such things as raglan and dolman sleeves, tailored collars, draped dresses etc. For these, continue to use that excellent product, the commercial paper pattern and if you want to make changes to it, at least you now know how to do it.

If you have enjoyed using this book and find it useful, and if you want to progress to more elaborate styles and more advanced patterns, well then I shall of course write a follow-up book to include just that.

Useful Addresses

Harlequin, Unit 25, Jubilee End, Lawford, Manningtree, Essex CO11 1UR.
Telephone: 0206–396167
Ann Ladbury's sewing tools and haberdashery, including spiked tracing wheels.

R.D. Franks Ltd, Kent House, Market Place, Oxford Circus, London W1.
Telephone: 01–636–1244.
Pattern drafting equipment and range of specialist fashion magazines.

McCulloch & Wallis, 25 Dering Street, London W1. Telephone: 01–629–0311.
Sewing and drafting equipment, haberdashery.